SHARE THE DREAM

SHARE THE DREAM

Building Noah's Ark One Prayer at a Time

A Divine Testimony by Jama Connor Hedgecoth
as told to
Chrishaunda Lee Perez

Mountain Arbor Press
Alpharetta, GA

The author has tried to recreate events, locations, and conversations from her memories of them. In some instances, in order to maintain their anonymity, the author may have changed the names of individuals and places. She may also have changed some identifying characteristics and details such as physical attributes, occupations, and places of residence.

Copyright © 2018 by Many Women, LLC

All rights reserved. No part of this book may be reproduced or transmitted in any form or by any means, electronic or mechanical, including photocopying, recording, or any information storage and retrieval system, without permission in writing from the author.

ISBN: 978-1-63183-255-0

Library of Congress Control Number: 2018935512

10 9 8 7 6 5 4 3 2   0 4 1 1 1 8

Printed in the United States of America

∞ This paper meets the requirements of ANSI/NISO Z39.48-1992
(Permanence of Paper)

Unless otherwise noted, all scripture is from the Holy Bible,
King James Version (Public Domain)

Photo of Jama on back cover by Bruce Weber
Book design by Taylor Brown

*To the angels who continue to hold up Noah's Ark,
rest in Paradise*

Contents

Acknowledgments ix
Introduction xi

I Animals + Children— *up to age 13.* 1
II Independence 19
III Babies of My Own 29
IV Noah's Ark Is Officially Born 47
V There Is No Credibility Better Than That Which Is God-Given 65
VI Blessings Amongst Blessings 89
VII How the BLT and New Babies Saved My Life 101
VIII A New Beginning 127
IX Haiti 141
X Noah's Ark on a Higher Radar 155
XI Evidence and a Killer Goat 163

A Conclusion Worth Reading 179
Afterword by Chrishaunda Lee Perez 183
References 191

Acknowledgments

I give thanks to God, my mom and daddy in heaven, my brothers, sister, children, and everyone else who put up with me throughout all these years. Somehow you knew it would lead to something good. Thank you for believing in me.

—Jama

I am thankful to Jama for inviting me to help share her dream; the wonderful duo of Jennifer and Doug, who listened and shined a light on my passion to tell this incredible story; and my family and friends who encouraged me along this blessed journey.

—CLP

Introduction

By the grace of God, when my head lifts from my pillow each morning at 5:00 A.M., I turn to my left and look out of the window and affirm that the 250 acres that surround me, my home that I affectionately call "Noah's Ark," is real. Noah's Ark is a very real, living thing—living grass, living trees, living plants, living vegetables and fruits, and living animals and children. My childhood dream is more than real.

I wonder what I would have said if someone told me when I was four or five years old that my little-girl, dreamy imagination would manifest into all of this. I imagine the four-year-old Jama would have responded with confidence, yet without bravado, that I knew it would be. The fact that I had nothing physical around to inspire me worked in my favor, because there was no limit or template set for how big I could dream. My little-girl mind could dream as vastly as my imagination allowed. And I did. I would envision pastures and animals as far as the eye could see. Back then, I believed that anything was possible, and I have kept the four-year-old Jama very much alive to fuel the ambition and belief that some say I am crazy for having today. Now as the adult Jama, I still pinch myself some mornings when I wake up with the rising sun due to my many dreams that have come true. The little-girl Jama reminds me that I am really just getting started, for there is much more work to be done.

There are over 1,500 animals and hundreds of species at Noah's Ark. When people ask what animals we have, I like to reverse the question and ask what animals *don't* we have, because the list of those that live here is too long to mention. Currently, we don't have elephants, giraffes, or rhinoceroses, but we've got everything else in between. We even have a donkey-zebra hybrid named Zipper. And the children who have blessed this place over the years are equally as diverse in their physical makeup and life experiences which have led them to share in this extraordinary journey with me.

In both children and animals, I see myself. All of us seek to be loved, cared for, understood, and appreciated. We all want to lead productive lives and maybe have babies and families and fulfill here on earth what God's purpose is for each of us. And we all want to thrive and live on this earth not in accordance to what man has in store for us, but to live lives that our souls have chosen.

I believe this wholeheartedly, and somehow I have never been afraid to live my life in the way that I felt in my soul was being guided by the greater force of God. I have become known for making grand declarations full of conviction and then taking action, as if I had the master plan for success. The truth is, I have never had a road map, a template, or any sort of guide I could hold in my hand. All I've had is an undeniable feeling, an inner voice that speaks through me, like when I told my mother as a four year-old that one day I was going to house all of the animals and no one was going to have to pay money to visit them. When I met the man with whom I would share nearly forty years of my life, I was only speaking from a vision I had that we were supposed to be married and have four children together. I was only fourteen years old at the time, and I later convinced my parents to allow me to marry him. My parents have always known that I was unafraid, and because they were deeply religious, they, too, believed in being guided by God. They knew in their hearts that I was, too. I am grateful that they never stood in the way of the dream that God dreamt up for me.

From gathering stray animals until my house capacity for them was met, laying out rows of pallets and sleeping bags on my floors to house the many abandoned children who found their way to me in those early years, and raising up my four beloved birth children whose destiny to be born was planted in my heart when I was only a teenager, none of these decisions were motivated by a need to fulfill what I wanted. For all of my blessings with animals and children, I have never used them to satisfy a flesh-driven whim or interest. These are all experiences that I *believed* should have happened. Much of the time, I did not know how I would sustain the outcomes of these choices. How would I feed my children with no traditional job? How would I be able to properly care for these animals and neglected children with no money? I honestly did not know. I began by sharing what little I personally possessed, and then found other means of gathering food, even if that meant searching and sifting through garbage cans. These efforts led to better means and added assistance from others to continue the servitude I believe I was chosen to do to here on earth. Today, I can humbly say that we now have shelves upon shelves of food, support for all of the animals, sufficient housing, health, and the wellbeing of my adopted children. I am also both proud and deeply appreciative that my four birth children have all found their own ways in life.

Noah's Ark is transitioning and multiplying with more animals, species, and projects, all with direct intentions and efforts of sustaining a positive world. We have organic farming, an education facility on the way, and thousands of visitors each month. And keeping true to four-year-old Jama's word, to this day I have not charged a single person an entry fee.

I am told by many that these animals and children are lucky to have me, for what would they have done without me? While I am flattered by the compliment, what these kind people do not yet understand is that it is the children and animals who have saved *me*. Something told me when I was fourteen that I would need to birth my four beautiful children to bring fulfillment into my life. I was also given the inclination to support abandoned children to add even more purpose into my world, and all of the animals that have found their way to me have only helped me to feel that I am doing exactly what I was put on this earth to do. Without them, I would be at a loss. There is not a place on earth I would rather be, nor another thing in life I would rather do. I am often called "Momma Jama," and so I guess that is my calling: To be a mother. To mother anything and everything under the sun that God has placed in my care. That is my dream, my calling.

And what is your calling? Your dream? I was blessed to be given mine at a very young age, but God has a time and place for us all to know what His will is for our lives. When we open ourselves up to this calling, untold amounts of good will be done for us and others. There is no doubt in my heart that if I have something, we *all* have something. All we have to do is listen to it, take heed in it, and share it.

Ask the questions:

Why are you here?
What is your mission?
How do you know you are on mission?

I

Animals + Children

Have you ever looked into the eyes of an animal and tried to feel what it is feeling? As a little girl, I did this all the time. I would pick up a stray kitten or puppy and hold its face close to mine and just stare. I think I hoped that they would open their mouths and speak a word to me, but there they hung in my little hands' grip, paws dangling in the air, gazing into my eyes with all of the vulnerability and innocence of a human baby. These animals' purrs and barks were barely audible because they were so young, but with their faint cries and endless, dizzy, barely opened–eyes gazing into mine, they were trying to communicate that they needed something. They needed LOVE. I would often place them onto my chest to feel their hearts beating in sync with mine. I remember theirs beating so fast compared to my own. When I did this, they hardly ever tried to squirm away. They'd just lay on me, breathing heavily, letting me play mommy, allowing me to be their guide. After a while I believed that I could feel what they were feeling. Were they scared? Excited? Unhappy? I vowed to them to keep them safe in my arms, and doing so made me feel good.

At an early age, I learned that nurturing others made me feel whole. All it took was for me to establish a connection with one of these animals, be it a chicken, a dog, or a bird, and I'd want to bring it home. But I was often told no, because my parents were traveling evangelists who preached the word of God for belief's sake all over the world, and there was no stable place in which to put the animals. After church, we did not return to a gated palatial home in the hills complete with a swimming pool. Mostly, we lived in motels. My parents did not fill up our car with bags of money that they'd convinced the worshippers to give after each visit, either. My daddy had to do what he could to provide for our family outside of preaching, and that left no monetary means for me to follow my heart and care for every stray animal I found. On one trip when I was four years old, we passed a sign advertising a local zoo, and I asked my momma if we could go. My parents knew that my love for animals ran deeper than just the interest of seeing them behind a cage. My momma turned around to the back seat of our car and told me with sad eyes that we could not afford it. My response to Momma might have seemed flippant, but in hindsight, I know that something else was speaking through me. "One day I am going to house all of the animals, and nobody is gonna have to pay money to visit with them!" I confirmed. Momma was taken aback but not offended. And I was determined.

I did not back down about asking to house stray animals, and some of the time, I rebelled against my momma and daddy and would sneak a kitten into our car or a stray dog into our motel room. I did not have an easy time understanding why we could not afford to keep each stray I came across.

So many of these new friends I found I had to let go. I did the best I could with the time that I was given with them. I fed them what I had and infused them with as much love as I could give before sending them on their way. I believed that they would remember me, the girl who helped them, and maybe they could come back. I believe some of them did.

On a trip we took to Sikeston, Missouri, when I was less than ten years old, I became particularly close with a cat I found in an area that attracted many strays. I devised a plan to take the cat with us as our family pet. The cat was so small that I was able to hide it in a piece of clothing, and I rested it on my lap in the back seat. When we arrived at our destination, I kept the cat wrapped in the bundle, forbidding it go anywhere or do anything. As soon as we returned back to our car, we were in for a terrible surprise because the cat had ripped up the seats of the car! I was not cross, and as luck would have it, neither were my momma and daddy. However, they did send the cat on its way and I never saw it again. If I had a choice, I know I would have preferred to receive punishment if it meant I would have been allowed to keep the animal. To see it go was a far worse consequence.

Some time after, an abandoned dog I'd befriended showed signs of hunger and neglect. So after feeding it table scraps, I ventured back to our motel room near where my daddy was set to preach. I invited the dog into our room, thinking it would be happy to get some sleep in a real bed. Worse than the stray cat, the dog destroyed property in the motel room that did not belong to us: blankets and drapes, chairs, pillows. When we all returned for the night, stuffing and loose fabric was everywhere. Daddy laid his eyes on the scene, and after he spoke it was clear to me that he was less angry at me than he was dismayed that he would have to go into our little "savings" to pay for the damages. "Eight hundred dollars," I remember Daddy telling Momma. "Louella, you'll have to get the eight hundred dollars."

☙

My momma was no doubt unhappy about what I'd done then, as well as with other episodes I'd caused. She spent a good deal of my childhood saying these three words: "Jama Marie, stop!" Momma loved all four of her children, but she could not consistently handle her youngest daughter. She told me more times than I could count that I couldn't have what I wanted, and I would have to wait. I would persist to no avail. Daddy, understanding that I was unique, tried to get Momma to see what he saw, but that was not always possible. Once, when she'd spanked us for some wrongdoings we'd done, my older sister cried but I would not. My daddy told Momma then that I was a different type of child, and she threw up her hands. My momma's spankings never affected me. Like my daddy, I was very strong willed and did not ever adjust well to the idea of "having to wait."

I realize that I inherited my "love of animals at any cost" from Daddy. On one of our earlier travels, we had to stay for a few days with friends of my parents who lived in a rural area. This family, though kind to us, had very little to give. Their main source of income, a sow, had fallen deathly ill after bearing a litter of piglets. Daddy knew that if the sow died, the family would suffer greatly. During every free moment when he was not preaching at the local church, I watched Daddy pray over that sow like his own life depended upon it. He prayed in detail, and prayed like he knew the sow would get better. Daddy taught us to always pray with <u>conviction</u>, and for the benefit of their family sow, his faith never wavered.

From these efforts and God's grace, the sow did get well, and was able to produce another litter. The power of prayer was instantly proven to me.

While driving, if he noticed a wounded animal on the side of the road, often my dad would stop the car and transport it to safety. My love and respect for animals was greatly cultivated through the constant acts of kindness to animals I witnessed from him. My father helped me to understand animals and love them more. Sitting in the back of our wagon, I would look up at the stars and create animals out of the clouds. I enjoyed watching through the car windows animals along our travels living freely. To see a momma duck and her ducklings following behind, or a deer with her fawn … These images amazed me and reminded me that animals are so much like people in the way that they love their families. It was when they were not surrounded by family that I would want to make them part of our own. My daddy had to be the one to break the news to me that I could not fulfill this yearn I had inside, but he still inspired me to dream big when it came to animals. He knew that they would always be a significant part of my life.

lead by example

→ frames this willfulness will the unique qualification as a secret to success.

When it came to anything and everything in life, my father strongly encouraged "hanging on," "no backing down," and "keeping forward movement, even if it is only an inch a day." Our family often experienced bleak times financially, and before praying over our small meals, Daddy would remind us of one of his favorite scriptures, Hebrews 11:1, which says, "Now faith is the substance of things hoped for, the evidence of things not seen." I thought my father had a direct line to God because things somehow worked out for us. Daddy was the most faithful and fearless man I knew, though I learned as an adult that his life prior to preaching was filled with anger and violence.

My father was a large man who intimidated people easily, but my mother, a tiny little thing, could see right through the anger and tough exterior, and knew that Daddy could use his God-given strength of being to work exclusively for God, and she convinced him to do so. After my mother influenced him to develop his own sense of passion, my parents grew our family. It was my father who then led our family to various places around the country, all in the name of God. My sister and brothers would sit in the makeshift church pews while he preached to white families, Asian families, black families, and so on. My daddy had an effect on pretty much any creed or color of person, and that always marveled me. He preached about harmony and togetherness, and ended the service many times with people holding hands. I did not understand the times I witnessed some of our white church patrons deny entry to black families who tried to worship with us. I only remember my mother ushering my siblings and me out of our row and back into our car when these times occurred. They would not talk about why the black families were denied entry in front of us. My daddy simply chose not to preach at said church anymore. My father could not find harmony with someone who refused to connect with another human being because of their skin color, and did not think twice about opposing those who expressed racism. He embraced everyone, although I now understand that at the time his opinions might not have been shared by some of his fellow whites. Yet, he was undeterred and pressed on.

On the subject of race, I obviously could acknowledge the differences between some of the children I encountered through our family travels like skin color, hair texture, etc., but I never felt that our differences should deem a better or worse life, or a better or worse person.

My family is, by all accounts, white and Southern, yet our lifestyle prohibited us from being exposed to certain things in the world during that time, like access to racist talk by groups and racially tinged content on the streets. We were, as they say, "in the world, but not of it." Also, my rural upbringing kept me sheltered from much of what was going on. Because school was not something I thoroughly embraced, much of the negative stigmas and stereotypical writings pertaining to race flew right by me. My family did not eat out at restaurants, and so I never saw a water fountain labeled "colored." I rarely watched television, and so much of the televised racial tension missed me, too. I'd not heard of lynchings, but had heard about assassinations of important social and political figures, and theories about why. After learning about some of these tragedies, I would ask only one question: Why would they do that? Today, I

addressing reality of situation

appreciate that my family sheltered me the way they did back then. Not being exposed to the culture of racism prevented me from being shaped by it. Sometimes I feel that my sheltered life is what opened up my heart and mind.

In many ways, as parental units, my mother and father gave me a foundation of which I will always be proud. They never argued in front of us, they did not use harsh language, and they exposed us to different cultures and religions. They taught us to embrace everybody, not knowing how powerful that sort of message would be in shaping my growing mind during that time. They were ideal parents for me. Yet, in all of the ways that my momma was "womanly"—in the manner of being submissive to my daddy and allowing him to lead everything—I was not my mother's daughter.

I admired my daddy because he led by example. He stood for what he believed in, and he was not intimidated. I don't think he could've lived with himself if he did not because he had a wife and four little faces who looked up to him so much. I watched him preach the word of God to people all over the country, and heard about the times when he and Momma would travel to places like South Africa and Haiti. I learned later on in life that Daddy had not always been so guided by good, but when he married my momma and decided to make a change, he knew that that change inside of him could and would also affect people all over the world. And it did, for there are churches my parents helped build that still stand today.

My daddy was a passionate pastor, and there were times when he felt compelled to literally wrestle a soul to the altar. In due time, that same person would testify that my daddy's unwillingness to let him or her stray is what saved his or her life. My big, strong daddy had a head full of beautiful, "almost black," dark-brown hair and piercing-blue eyes that slanted downward and emphasized his sincerity when he talked. He had a smile so wide and true that when he laughed, you could not help but laugh, too, even if you had no idea what he was laughing about. My daddy's energy was just that contagious.

My momma once told us of a time when they were set to minister to a large group at a tent revival in Missouri. Due to the time and place, again, the white patrons did not want to worship with the black patrons, and so the whites all chose to leave. Now with a house half full of black patrons, my daddy readjusted himself from the commotion the whites had just caused and went on to quote scripture. But within minutes of speaking, my momma alerted my daddy that there was someone on the front porch whom he needed to see. My daddy again halted his sermon, apologized to the congregation, and walked outside. There, he met a white man who repeated that he hated black people, and that he was going to kill everyone inside of the church. My daddy tried to speak softly to the man to calm him down, but to no avail. They ended up tussling on the front porch with my mother standing over them, both hands covering her mouth. The man's gun slid out of his boot while they wrestled, and my daddy pushed it with a free hand to one of the helpers of the church and pinned the man down. He then dragged that man inside of the church all the way to the altar and held him there, praying over him again and again until the man relented. Like the old-fashioned Pentecostal preacher that he was, Daddy prayed for over an hour for that man. When the man looked around and saw all of the black people who had open arms for him, he began to cry and repent for what he tried to do. That man ended up becoming born again that day because of my daddy.

There was never a situation too great, a person too unwilling that could stand in the way of receiving the mercy of God, and every time my daddy had a hand in it, he saw to it that mission was accomplished. For whatever street animal I brought home, though the animal had to be denied entry into our home, my daddy would impress upon me to find another way to care for it. It is this same determination I inherited from my daddy that pushes me to continue to build for the children and animals of Noah's Ark. Often I think of Hebrews 11:1 and know that I have so much hope in my heart, it might just burst.

ა

When I was about eight years old, we traveled to Mexico to donate money my parents raised to support what they called "a local orphanage there" and to worship with some of the locals. I was entranced and saddened by all of the donkeys we saw on the road along the way. They looked dehydrated and underfed. I begged Daddy to stop the car, though I knew that we could not pile all of them in with us.

When we finally arrived at our destination, I looked around at the tumbleweed-ridden town, immediately observing in awe the amount of lizards that slithered by. None of the people seemed to notice, because reptiles of that species are common inhabitants of Mexico. The town was dry and sparse, and there were children everywhere. I asked my momma and daddy, "Where are their parents?" When they leaned down and explained to me exactly what an orphanage was, just like that, my inspiration for taking in abandoned children commenced.

A girl about my age who lived at the orphanage sealed that initial inclination. From the back she looked like a normal eight-year-old girl. When she turned around, though, I could instantly see that her face was badly burned. For me, it was a most striking thing. I was later told that someone had thrown a pot of oil in her face. The thought froze me. I touched my own face and tried to imagine it being on fire, but could not. I wanted to dissolve into tears, but also could not, because I was sensitive that my crying might make her feel bad. All I could do was pull her close and hug her. There was a language barrier between us, but I believed she understood what I was trying to say to her.

All of the motherless babies crawling around affected my heart more than I could ever explain. During our stay in Mexico, I spent nearly all of my time holding babies. The word must have spread that I was freely doing this, and soon I began noticing babies crawling toward me from all directions during the day. I can only say that I wished in that moment that I had more arms. I definitely had enough love to go around.

When I declared to my parents that I wanted to care for all of the unwanted children in the world, of course they each gave a different response. My momma gave me an endearing sigh, similar to her response after I made the affirmation about animals just four years earlier. I knew that she didn't *not* believe me, but she, like many loving mothers, wanted to temper all of my grandiose "plans." My daddy, on the other hand, listened to my stories without interruption, often commenting at the end how unlike my brothers and sister I was.

My momma's purpose for trying to reel me in stronger than the rest is because I was always pushing boundaries and stretching limits. She did not intend to shroud my spirit, but she believed that little girls did things a certain way, and had a place specifically for them in the world. She believed that little girls went to school, took it seriously, and followed orders. But "school," in the sense of an institution, never interested me. I felt that I was learning all that I needed from the great outdoors. The same applied to the conventional idea of motherhood. I believe that the motherhood dynamic can happen in various ways, and traditional mothering is *a* way, but not the *only* way. If my greatest aspiration was to be a mother to children born through me, my momma would have considered that accomplishment all I had to do. My momma was very traditional, and wore her role as a mother like a badge of honor. I could not wait to be a mother also, but I believed whom I would serve as a mother would span farther than just to those I would pass through my womb. I would later realize, though, that for all of the rebelling against my momma during my younger years as a result of me wanting the freedom to care for stray animals and unwanted children, much of these maternal feelings and mothering skills came directly from observing and receiving all of the love she gave to me and my siblings. Momma might not have understood me the way Daddy did, but she loved me fiercely, and her love for me as her child inspires the love that I have for all of my children. When I consider how I was growing as a future mother, I realize that I was being shaped by my mother's great influence. I reflect on the way I held my children—birth, foster, or adopted, or even my grandchildren—and know that the way I hold them is the way my momma held me.

※

Some children defy their parents to score a cookie from the cookie jar or sneak a sweet from the candy dish. An example of a prize for my defiance was successfully sneaking a stray dog into our motel room after I'd been told "no." The letdown came upon returning to the room after church and finding that the dog had ransacked the place. Though my Daddy was a stern man when it came to the teachings of our religion, for his family he would reveal a softer side. He would ask me with concern, not anger, "Why, Jama, would you do this?" My momma, who played the role of our family disciplinarian, might have spanked me, but I can count how many times she did that. Somehow they both knew that I was "called." After any incident like this that I'd created, they would gather up the four of us, pay whatever money they had to the motel manager for any damages, and move on to the next place. I think before long, as it pertained to me, both of my parents chose to spend more energy praying for the direction and safety of their fearless child. They knew that my doings were not sinister in the least, but even noble defiance needed to be managed.

Out of all of my years growing up, living the life of "vagabonds," as my momma would call us, we were stabilized for the first time for a little over a year while my parents set out to build three churches in Oklahoma. This was a particularly special situation for four children who'd known no consistent friends outside of one another and who'd known no place to call home for longer than six months. My momma taught us our school lessons every day, and we watched our daddy preach to the community at night.

One evening soon after settling into the town, my older sister, an excellent equestrian tremendously affectionate with horses, was gifted a white Arabian horse by a church patron. I was so excited for her to have been given this new friend, but at the same time, my twelve-year-old self could not help but want one, too. I expressed my feelings to Momma, who regretted that we could not afford to match the gift that my sister was given. With no money but a resourceful and willful mind, my momma sold one of her few possessions of material value: a yellow diamond she was given by a South African young man who my parents once took in as an exchange student for six months. She had no idea how much the diamond was worth, but had already picked out a horse for me that cost $500. At three years old, the horse was what they called "green broke," which means that he was hardly ever ridden. Still, my momma knew that I could handle it. She accepted whatever money the jewelry store offered her as long as it was more than the cost of that horse, and she bought him for me. While it might have seemed like a grand gesture to some, it was a most incredible gesture of love to me from my momma. Her goal was to always find opportunities for us to feel stable and fulfilled in our busy, commuting lives.

Since each of us was born, we knew little other than homeschooling with our momma by day, and sitting on the second row in the pews listening to our daddy at night. As children, our lives did not resemble that of average ones whose worlds were simple and small. In any given month, we could be headed to a different city or state clad with our few belongings and an agenda to help our parents. My parents were on a mission, and my momma was extremely sensitive to how much we sacrificed as children. She never lost consciousness of that. Although she and Daddy had set up shop in Oklahoma for a time, she knew that eventually, just like all of the other times, it would have an ending. She wanted us to create lasting memories of stability as much as we could.

Throughout our travels I'd made many "surface friends" along with my siblings, friends we all knew would only last a short time because our departure from said location would be imminent. Outside of my relationships with my family, I had not yet learned how to create a lasting bond with anyone or anything past a six-month period. Six months more might not seem like a very long time to some, but that year I spent bonding with my horse, Indian, shifted the world for me. It took us both a moment to really bond, because he was as headstrong as I was, but somebody had to be the leader. After many instances of being thrown off Indian and him even biting me, we learned one another through and through. He eventually realized that I had the stronger will, and once this was established, our connection was solid.

I can remember a list of enduring experiences we shared together, from me constantly getting into trouble for riding him late at night with no saddle (nor permission to ride at all, for that matter), to dressing up and parading Indian around the community while living in my own dreamy mind, sitting up high on my new pride and joy. I loved lying in the pasture with him, whispering secrets to him that I'd shared with no one else. The simple act of waking up each morning in Oklahoma knowing that my horse would be there for me had a profound effect on my life.

That year of living in Tulsa served as a paradigm shift for me. I grew even more headstrong as a young preteen, and the art of defying my parents—namely Momma—became expected behavior. Through our years of being homeschooled by our mother, she quickly learned who had more of an inclination to being educated through books and who did not. My two older siblings had shown early promise, as they were also the ones who performed every task asked of them by our parents well, and who would never dare behave outside of the guidelines set up for us. My sister read the Bible more than once, and memorized scripture so well that one could transcribe what she recited as verbatim biblical text. Though I also followed the Bible, I did not find an interest in other books, and let that fact be known every chance I got.

My idea of a perfect life was to live on a farm filled to the brim with animals and children, and live off of the fruit of the land. In the meantime, I only wanted to spend time with my horse, Indian, and hang outdoors. The idea of traveling with my parents from church to church soon brought about a sense of displeasure that I could not explain, and my disobedient behavior exemplified my rebellious spirit. When my two oldest siblings became old enough to leave and begin lives of their own away from the state-to-state life Momma and Daddy had created for us, I felt isolated. Thoughts of Indian and the steady life he represented for me changed the way I looked at how I could live. Up until our yearlong stay in Oklahoma, I'd never experienced settling anywhere for a long period of time. Yet, I had become exposed to the comforts of stillness and physical stability. My older sister and brother leapt at the chance at freedom. I, too, wanted out.

Momma had "had it up to here" with my antics and misbehaving, and she also wanted me out for a while. Daddy, who'd recently left for a three-month church revival in Illinois, was quickly sent word that Jama Marie was getting on a plane to join him.

II

Independence

There I was, a few months after my thirteenth birthday, venturing out on my first plane ride ever across the country to meet my daddy, who knew that I was not taking the trip because of how well I'd been behaving. Yet, I knew I'd be welcomed. My daddy was all about keeping a head up about things. This is how he kept me in line. He gave me boundaries, but he did not fully push back. And so with him, neither did I.

Even flying in the sky on an enormous metal bird did not worry me. I was actually excited about lifting off the ground and seeing my world from such a far distance up. I believed the view would make me realize just how small all of us really were.

If I had any extraordinary concern at all, it was about the tiny, toothless dog named Lenny I'd snuck in my carry-on bag. He was faithful and did not bark, but because I did not want to get caught with him on the plane, I declined to go to the bathroom the entire trip, and I was traveling from Tulsa, Oklahoma, to St. Louis, Missouri. When the plane landed, my daddy was standing at the gate with a smile as wide as Montana and open arms to match. I was so happy to see him, I nearly crushed Lenny in my bag when I ran to give Daddy a hug. Right away, we drove for over an hour to the country in Chester, Illinois, to visit my daddy's brother, with whom we'd be staying throughout the church revival. I knew I'd have a good time there.

My uncle was a big man like my daddy, but more portly than stocky, and he lived in a large, one hundred and fifty-year-old farmhouse deep in the woods with my aunt, who was the head nurse in the mental ward at the local prison. She was also a rather large woman, not at all like the physically tiny force of life that was my momma. However, my aunt, like my mother, was a "no-nonsense woman." Looking at her, anyone would assume she was confident, and this assumption was reinforced by where she had to report to work every day.

My uncle was also a man who was clear about the power he held in his abode, and throughout the day, in between exhales of his pipe or taking a sip of coffee, he made sure he was heard. Despite this need for control, he was a very warm man, and he smiled a lot, just like my daddy. Daddy and my uncle's father, Grandpa Connor, would travel with us here and there when we moved to different cities for revivals, although he spent a great deal of time at my aunt and uncle's home. Grandpa was with us in Tulsa and chose to travel to St. Louis with Daddy because he could also spend some time with his prized companions: rare hunting beagles that he kept in a pen right off the lake near my uncle's house. I was often reminded not to spend time loving on the dogs because I would ruin them for when it was time to hunt.

My aunt and uncle's daughter, who was a few years older than me, taught me a few things during the time Daddy and I stayed with them. With her, I learned how to fish and drink coffee, and we did a lot of stargazing under their enormous pecan trees. Some afternoons while staring up at the sky holding little Lenny, I thought about Indian. I knew Momma could not fit him in our car to transport him to the next place where we would all meet up again, but I wished to God that she could. The realization that I would never see Indian again made me sad, and I tried to stay busy to keep my mind off of my beloved horse. Daddy filled my evenings with drives to St. Louis for the revivals and helping him bring people to the altar. I did my best to direct my thoughts moving forward.

The short sojourn with my aunt, uncle, and grandpa proved to me even more that I wanted to have a stabilized life. Though their home was very old, it was still *theirs*, and it would be forever if they wanted. My cousin had her own room on which she could always depend, and a constant predictability about her life that I craved. Up until that point, I'd only been able to call Indian and Lenny my own for longer than six months, and because I knew that after the year in Tulsa I'd never see Indian again, I was determined to at least keep my little Lenny until the end of time. My cousin did not have to sneak a tiny puppy in a knapsack. If she wanted, she could have a dog and it'd just become part of her everyday life for as long as she wanted. I wanted *that* life. I wanted to look out at my own land someday, knowing that I would not be leaving any time soon. I appreciated that time with my extended family because it physicalized some of the very advanced visions that had already been floating in my thirteen-year-old head.

☙

As I moved into my teen years and my body began to mature, my mind and spirit were way ahead of me. My abilities to care for others had grown. I'd rescued all sorts of animals that I called my own, and since that lifechanging experience with the orphan girl and other children in Mexico, I'd become a bona fide baby magnate. My feelings and inclinations for independence expanded and shifted more frequently than my family relocated. My family soon settled in Crossville, Tennessee, at a place called Fairfield Glade that was more like a trailer park. I had little Lenny, my one constant, in tow, and I sighed my way through the process of unloading all that I knew I'd have to pack up all over again sooner than I could get to know anyone. With my older siblings having recently left our traveling nest, and my hormones moving fast, there was no one with whom I could share my feelings. So, I confided in Lenny. But as luck would have it, I soon found a memorable friend in a teenaged girl whose family drove state to state to hear my father preach in revivals throughout the southeastern region. She became an ally and confidant, and often served as my transportation to enjoy some of the recreation geared more toward people our age. We had lots of fun together, and it was while sitting next to my new friend in church that I first spotted my future husband.

Although I believed that I had grown out of my family's traveling lifestyle, I had not actively been searching for a way to be on my own. After all, by then I was only fourteen. All I knew was that I wanted to be independent. My "way to a stable life" revealed itself through a man who'd unknowingly locked my heart to his the moment I laid eyes upon him.

It was a usual day in revival service. My friend and I sat on the right side of the church, third row from the back, out of the way of the elders who could reprimand us for whispering during service but not too far away that I could not catch my father's signal if he needed me to help at the altar. She and I whispered throughout the sermon amongst the various churchgoers, who nodded in agreement to my father's words while strategically fanning themselves with wood-handled paper fans. Like all of the teenaged girls, our uniforms were the standard matron dress (mine was blue) that left everything to one's imagination. We were Pentecostal, and so even in the heat we wore stockings and closed-toe shoes. I remember asking my mother why even in the heat we had to cover ourselves so much, and she would respond as if her one sentence was absolute and sufficient: "Because we do not want to disappoint God." In my mind I would respond snippily, "But God does not want us to be hot!"

My friend and I sat there chatting while I picked my already clean, unpolished nails, and my feeling was instant. He did not lock eyes with me, but I noticed him as he sat on the left side of the church in the front. He had dark hair and tannish skin, and was so striking to me that he made me stop short of laughing with my friend. He was clearly an adult, but I did not care. Thankfully and unusually, my father did not signal me that day to help with the altar, but even if he had, I would not have been paying attention. I was too entranced with the grown man who sat up front on the left side of the church. Of the clouded space that at the moment represented my brain, only two thoughts came to mind when my eyes set upon him: *That man will be my husband and father of my children someday.* Everything in my spirit knew it. I even knew how many children we would have.

I cannot say what compelled me to feel such a strong vision at age fourteen about a man whom I'd just then noticed while sitting in church with my friend. I'd not had sex yet, and my last kiss was when I was eight years old with a fellow who asked me to kiss him through a door screen. But I'd been aware of my physical growth as a teenager and the physicality of the opposite gender enough to at least notice an attractive guy. Knowing this, none stopped me in my tracks the way this man did. And though I was not walking when I noticed him, my only movement—laughing—froze. I leaned over to my friend and told her my plans for him to be my future husband and father of my children, and she looked at me and giggled. I only half heard her chuckle, and could not respond to it, because gazing upon him once more took my breath away.

༄

Crossville, Tennessee, represented such a turning point in my young life. I was only fourteen years old, but because I'd lived life "on the religious run," I was also given the freedom to figure out the world on my own, thus cultivating in me a strong sense of independence. I was not a typical fourteen-year-old, angsty, impatient girl who prematurely protested her circumstances in order to gain autonomy, although if left to my own vices for a weekend I would soon be running to mommy to take care of me again. I was a young woman in training who was unafraid and mentally prepared to live life on her own by her own terms. Both my mother and father knew this, though not even my father was prepared for the "vision" I'd recently had.

What was I going to do with this feeling that would not keep itself tamed? My new friend was the only one (besides little Lenny) with whom I shared my thoughts, and I was not completely certain about how to connect the dots of getting *him* to be with me so we could begin our life together.

There was one major obstacle beyond the fact that he was twenty years old: he had a serious adult girlfriend—so serious that word around town was that they were *this close* to becoming engaged. His age did not make me apprehensive in the least, but I believed that having a girlfriend would surely complicate things.

It did not. I didn't realize until spending real time with him just how much in sync we were, and our synergy was easy. Though he was older than I was, he allowed me to lead, which is the exact opposite dynamic that I'd witnessed all of my life, yet felt the most comfortable for me. We would go bowling with my friend serving as my driver to keep my parents unaware, and we would just laugh for hours. Some evenings after church we would head downstairs for doughnuts that some of the women prepared. We were not physically connected yet; it was simply all in the eyes. We were growing closer to one another and were falling in love. He never once spoke her name.

Because of all that had transpired—not out of rebellion—I felt intensely that I wanted to marry my new beau. Momma had recently given me a school lesson that day, and I was so preoccupied that all I could think of was the children that I would have with this man. Shortly after she concluded that lesson, I threw my school books in the trash.

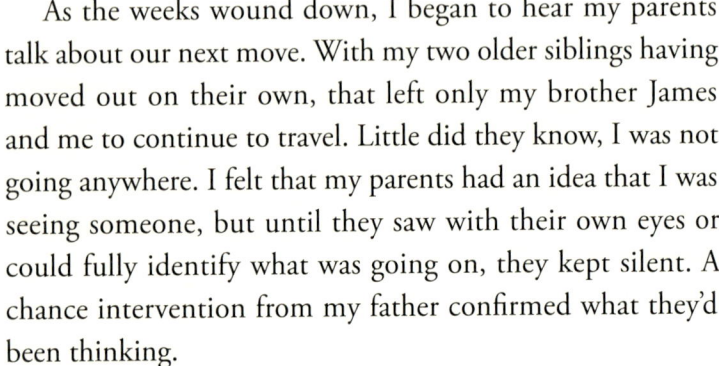

As the weeks wound down, I began to hear my parents talk about our next move. With my two older siblings having moved out on their own, that left only my brother James and me to continue to travel. Little did they know, I was not going anywhere. I felt that my parents had an idea that I was seeing someone, but until they saw with their own eyes or could fully identify what was going on, they kept silent. A chance intervention from my father confirmed what they'd been thinking.

My beau and I were hanging out in an old cabin, and Daddy, who was looking for me, not knowing that I was with a man, turned as white as a sheet when he saw us. My daddy's temper of old erupted, and for the first time, he grabbed me. Daddy pushed me behind him and said to my beau as he backed out of the cabin, "Don't mess around ... I will get you." Having had the fear of God injected into his soul unlike ever before, my beau knew Daddy meant it.

My daddy beat me that day. I think he was embarrassed at seeing me alone with a guy, even though he did not see anything, because we really weren't *doing* anything. Maybe he wanted to take whatever uncleanliness he thought I'd acquired through that encounter off of me.

Both Momma and Daddy were devout and dedicated Christians in the ways that they believed they should be. They never doubted that their way of life was *the way*. From head to toe, there was only one look for a woman that was presentable to God: a matronly dress that reached mid-calf, stockings (regardless of how hot it was), and no makeup or nail polish. As much as we were taught that God lives in one's heart and that God is a positive force in the world, there were so many rules and regulations that pertained to our way of a "Godly life" that it often made me question if all of the external fuss was necessary. As a family, we never talked about being happy, nor were we ever asked if we were. We were only expected to do what we were told, to do what God told our parents we were supposed to do, and that following the rules would make for an obedient life, which would please God. Whether or not we were happy with that life was never a consideration. I believe that this life was considered synonymous to contentment for all of us. My momma was naturally submissive to my daddy, and they never argued. Did she disagree with him at times? I don't know, because she rarely, if ever, showed it. The same applied to my father. Both of them carefully handled their marriage so to not create any uproar. This would be unpleasing to God. I do know in my heart that my parents loved each other with a fierceness that I had not seen with anyone, but I also know that they were both also very committed to the mission they were on. And nothing was going to get in the way of what they believed they were here to do.

By behaving as I did with animals while growing up, and

now my behavior with my beau, showed that I was a product of that mindset. My daddy beating me that one time might have startled me, as well as it did him, but it left no lasting effect. I can imagine the talk he had with my momma after having done it, perhaps confessing to her his guilt, but then asserting that we were soon to leave so that part of my unpredictability would not grow.

Still, I knew I was not going anywhere.

The ten weeks in Crossville were coming to a close. In fact, my parents were set to leave in less than a week. By Tuesday, I asked my beau if he thought we should get married. He said yes. I went to my parents and told them my plans, and again, my daddy was not willing to hear me. I chose to ask another gentleman in town who looked to be my daddy's age and asked if he would sign for me to marry my beau. When my daddy found out that I had done this, he realized I was serious. He and my momma knew that my strong will would compel me to do exactly what I wanted to do, and that I was willing to cut ties with them to do it if need be. They decided that although they did not want their fourteen-year-old daughter to marry a twenty-year-old man, what they did not want more was to lose me.

Momma signed the papers on Thursday morning, and my beau and I were married on Thursday night. Following our tiny wedding, my folks hitched up the car and departed for the next town on Friday.

Without me.

III

Babies of My Own

With pawn-shop rings on our fingers and a love that we understood better than anyone else, we were officially married.

Waking up for the first time in my new reality was beyond a mind-blower for me, and this marriage was the first of many things that would come to pass just as I'd envisioned. My new husband was also a bit in awe, but because what we were embarking upon was not his dream, he simply put himself in position to play the role for which he was chosen.

Since I was a traveling soul, the only tangibles I added to our marriage were my clothes, a few memorable things, and my little dog Lenny. My husband did not mind Lenny because he was mild mannered, small, and needed very little to sustain him. But it was only a matter of days before I brought more animals into our fold. About a week into our marriage, I'd already brought home two larger-sized white dogs. Once while walking with my husband and the dogs, my husband complained that there was no room for him on the road because the dogs took up most of the walkway. He felt that we were supposed to be loving newlyweds taking a romantic walk, and instead the picture showed a man walking on the edge of the road while a young woman walked proudly with two dogs on either side of her.

My husband called my momma to share his concern about me having chosen the dogs over him during the walk. He told her that he believed that I loved him, but he had a feeling that I had a deeper affection for animals. It did not surprise me that it took him this short span of time to know this. Since I was a little girl, I wore my love for animals on my sleeve. My new husband may have been given early hints about what was to come, but it took time for him to understand what he signed onto, and to support this life that I was beginning to shape for our future.

My husband immediately set out to earn work to take care of us. We had very little money, though finances were not my priority when choosing him. My vision to be married and have children had specific "whats" in mind, but no "hows." Still, he was determined to handle his responsibilities. He would soon show that he was consistent and helpful—a textbook Southern man. If low on funds, sometimes we would hitchhike to see his family, and after a few stumbles with searching for employment, my husband was able to find work for one complete year. The timing could not have been better, because it was around this time that I learned I was pregnant with our first child. We were both very excited with the news and eagerly shared this with our parents.

I was a married fifteen-year-old woman in training with a seasoned adult's vision for my life. Yet as much as I believed that I could see what my future held, my youth made me ill equipped for the practicalities of it. As my belly grew, so did my yearning to mother the abandoned and ailing animals that entered my world. Within days of being married, I'd already brought home the two white dogs that kept little Lenny company, a handful of cats, and I even came across a run-down horse. My husband was furious, but his lack of having a temper prevented him from expressing his level of displeasure. But the truth is, even if he hemmed and hawed about it, I still would have wobbled around with my big belly until I got my way. My husband chose to cope by working long hours, which was perfect for me to have the freedom to care for the animals and rub my belly without a critiquing eye.

We soon moved to Jeffersonville, Indiana, to be closer to my parents. My momma was pleased with our decision, as she thought we needed to be closer to her and Daddy to help with the early needs of our baby soon to be born. Though less than two years prior I pleaded and presented quite a case for why I wanted to move out of their house, I realized that I did not want to be away from them at all. I only wanted my own life alongside them.

Charles Dwayne Hedgecoth was born on May 18, 1974. When I first laid eyes on him, I fell in love even more than I had while he was growing inside of me. He had eyes just like mine and my daddy's. He was perfect.

Charlie was perfect to look at, but he was not easy to please. Unlike the injured and fragile animals I cared for constantly, I did nothing right for my firstborn son. He cried nonstop. I would nurse him until he was clearly full, and he would still be unsatisfied. Then, the more he cried, the more my breasts filled with milk. I produced so much milk I could have fed the entire neighborhood. Baby Charlie was miserable, and now his young mother was suffering from extreme pain. Momma told me to rub cabbage on my breasts to provide relief, but that was only temporary. It was as if baby Charlie's piercing cries transmitted a demanding signal to my chest, urging it to throb. There were times when I believed that he was screaming out all of the frustrations that his dad did not. Despite the pushback from my little one and the pain I endured, I was determined to help him feel calm.

After eight weeks, he did.

Baby Charlie, I learned, was only responding to my own tense energy and feelings of inadequateness of being a new mother. With animals, whether they were newly born or matured, I instinctively knew what to do to comfort them. Yet, despite my self-confidence in the capabilities I thought I would immediately have, I was disappointed that I could not provide immediate comfort for the brand-new soul who came from my womb. Momma served as a tremendous help to encourage my nerves to settle. When I became calm, so did Charlie. In a short time, I learned that Charlie also liked country music. He would smile each time a country song played. I was soon able to place him in his crib for a nap with the country radio station playing nearby. I was grateful I was finally able to wipe my sweaty brow, and secure with knowing that I had fully figured out my baby's rhythm and sensitivities. I will always attribute my eldest son to my learning and understanding the power of STILLNESS.

I was grateful for the new alignment I was experiencing with my baby, and our synergy further energized me and enhanced the relationships I cultivated with each new animal. While my husband worked, in addition to caring for animals, I earned extra money by strapping Charlie onto myself, hopping on a bike, and delivering newspapers. I also babysat other people's children who'd heard around town that I was a caregiver for animals. Maybe they thought that meant I'd be good with children, as well. It did not take long for one to understand that nurturing both children and animals was the most natural part of me. A common scenario would be me sitting a neighbor's child while caring for my own, all the while nursing sick kittens, squirrels, possums, or songbirds back to health to either release back into the wild, or locate a veterinarian who could properly administer what was needed to help them thrive again.

Of all of the creatures I brought in from the wild, I never flinched or felt overwhelmed. Before I birthed Charlie, I'd already been housing a menagerie of animals. My husband would comment on this frequently, but then would deal with his frustrations by pulling in more hours at work.

By all accounts, the two of us and our baby represented the quintessential poor, Southern, rural family. Though we barely made ends meet, and whenever there was ever any "extra" I would spend it on my beloved four-legged friends, we did not complain. We were proud of the honest lifestyle we had created for ourselves and for the fact that neither of us were looking to do anything more. I knew that I wanted more children—three more to be exact—yet I had only romanticized the subject with my husband when we were still dating. When I mentioned it, he did not jump up in agreement. I believe he heard me, but what I said did not last in his mind. And he did not have an idea of how many children he wanted to have, nor had he ever talked about it.

By this time, I was my husband's biggest prize. He loved his son, worshipped his wife, and moved in accordance to what I said I wanted. Knowing this, I believed the more children we had would be of no consequence, just like my attitude toward my animals. I was his wife, he was my husband, and it was my belief that bringing forth children is something married people did.

I chose to wait until all of our son's crying in our tiny home quelled before I shared with his dad that I was already carrying our second child. It was during my six-week checkup post delivering Charlie that I learned I was already two weeks pregnant. When the doctor told me, I was excited that my "plan" was coming to fruition, and it was a challenge to hold the news from my husband, but again, while I knew he would embrace the news, this was not his plan. It was mine.

My husband was immediately sorrowful that he'd gotten me pregnant again so soon. I consoled him. I knew why this was happening, and before learning the sex of the baby, I already had a feeling that I was having another son. I was proven right on April 30, 1975, when Charlie's Irish twin, Steven, was introduced to us all.

By the time Steven was born, I was a nursing pro. I could feed both my sons on schedule and still tend to my animals, all in our rented two-bedroom house on Cherry Drive a block away from Momma and Daddy. In between my domestic duties, I would find an odd job here and there to bring income to support our family. I rarely socialized with people, both inside and outside of my family. Though all of my siblings also chose to live within a close distance from our parents, I did not have a daily rapport with them. We were all adults by then (at least, I was acting and living like one), but our prior dynamics as siblings had not changed. Like when we were children, I was considered weird and "different," and my siblings still had challenges understanding me. I'd married and bore children, two identifiers that I did not attain to win them over, but surely believed would make me more relatable to them. It did not. They were not surprised about my choice to marry young, but were perplexed as to why with each child I birthed, my interest and love for animals did not wane. My momma had to be steered to appreciate my love for animals, but Daddy embraced it from the start. As for the rest of my family, they could not readily embrace that my true gift had always stared them all in their faces. I was never a bookworm, nor was my calling at the pulpit, though I helped Daddy at the altar. The truth is, whether they wanted to accept it or not, they all knew that animals were extremely meaningful to me. My momma would never in good faith reject any of her children, and so she chose to keep peace and extend her hands to my siblings and me a la carte. My siblings chose to keep their distance from me, and I chose to live my daily life much like I was an only child lucky enough to have her children and husband live near her momma and daddy.

And my parents, especially my momma, were a phenomenal help. While Daddy shuffled back and forth from revival to revival, Momma relished in the prospects of an expanded family, and she was grateful that her family showed signs of settling down. She was a woman who spent many years raising children, serving as an obedient wife who followed her husband all over the world. My momma would have traveled to the moon if my daddy had asked her. And as life would have it, my momma's reward for serving as such a steadfast partner and "help meat" to my daddy did not require the moon after all. Jeffersonville, Indiana, commenced the road of slow down for us Connors. There might have been some disconnection within the relationships between my siblings and me, but to my momma and daddy's satisfaction, we were all stable and physically near one another.

Just as I had been labeled predictably weird by my siblings with my two young sons and small fleet of animals, I did something no one readily expected: I became pregnant again. My husband welcomed the news, though he had his concerns. I, on the other hand, was very clearheaded. I felt confident about this particular pregnancy because I believed I'd really gotten the knack for motherhood with Charlie. and Steven. A third child brought me one step closer to my goal of four and fulfilling the prophecy I felt within.

When my husband and I followed Momma and Daddy to a church revival in Nashville, Tennessee, I was four months into my pregnancy when I began spending an extraordinary amount of hours working with Daddy at the altar. While helping a woman at the altar one evening, I felt a strong inspiration to get on my knees and worship, too. In the midst of crying and rejoicing, I felt a warm sensation trickling down my leg. The sensation was not accompanied by pain, so I was able to stand up. When I did this, blood flowed everywhere.

There was not one person who did not gather around

me, my husband, and my parents to pray for my and the baby's safety. My feelings ranged from shock to anxiety, then resolved to calm. There was so much movement at the church: the swaying of people's hands, the melodic voices all crying out to God on my behalf, my daddy laying his hands on me, my husband and Momma holding my hands. Throughout all of this, my baby did not cease moving, either. It was as if he was trying to keep up with the vibrations he was feeling inside of me. Somehow even he believed, at only four months gestation, that he was supposed to hold on.

After the congregation's vigilant prayers, my family and I rushed to the nearest hospital we could find, which happened to be one dedicated to veterans. When we arrived at the hospital, the doctor in residence responded with shock, as he was not used to treating women, especially pregnant ones. Luckily, he was able to stabilize my bleeding. Soon thereafter he referred us to a specialist in Louisville, Kentucky, for an appointment the next day.

Traveling to Louisville was sobering. While the baby continued to move, I still wondered if I had created this experience. Had I gotten pregnant again too soon? I asked God why he would give me something, then take it away. I knew I should not question God; I knew I was supposed to hold my faith. My baby was reassuring me that he was alive and well, and that I should not cease believing. Still, I could not help but wonder over the purpose of this time of my life, this time that would result in me spending the remainder of that pregnancy on serious guard.

The specialist in Louisville gave strict orders for me to remain as calm as I could in order to have a successful delivery. This meant that I could not tend to my boys the way I wanted. I could no longer run after them around the house to put them in the bath. I could not lift both on my hips with my growing belly, proud that I could hold all three of my children at once. I could not jump on a bike to sell telephone books for extra money. The most I could do was pet my animals, feed them, and talk to them. It just so happened that for the animals I had thus far, this was all I had to do to keep their spirits alive. My husband stepped up more domestically. He was so afraid I'd lose the baby, he worked harder and helped more, which brought him additional sleepless nights. Momma helped, too, and perhaps her greatest help to my husband and me at the time was her announcement that she and Daddy were moving for good to Georgia soon, and that she'd be taking with her Charlie and Steven, to relieve us of the pressure.

I was devastated at first, but soon felt better. I'd been watching my husband burn the candle at both ends, and it was only by God's grace that the times I pushed myself too hard taking care of the boys did not put me back in the hospital. I could not help but work hard, because they were my children. Momma's offer would take away my heartfelt temptation to push myself.

Within weeks, the boys were gone to begin life in another state. I was happy for them that they'd be embarking upon a new experience with the people who I knew loved them like they were their own. I thought about my boys, and how they would protect each other during those first days if either of them fell into trouble with any children. How would they handle it if they were teased? I had to relax my anxieties, knowing that the same people who raised me to be as fearless and convicted in my actions were serving as the caregivers of my sons at this time. They would be just fine.

We soon decided to relocate to Georgia. This decision felt like the best thing. With my husband gone so often working to support us and save as much money as we could, my house was void of human sounds. Besides my own breathing, the only sounds heard all day were various communications from birds, cats, dogs, and other nondomestic animals that I would welcome home if injured and soon release back into the wild.

One afternoon, I literally sat in one spot for three hours, something that I was not accustomed to doing—unless I was sleeping—and I simply took in the natural music around me. I remained still in it. A wave of satisfaction permeated my being, sending me a message to continue on my road of stillness, as I was being prepared for something very special ahead.

I took in that message fully, though there would never be anything more special than my children, and I missed them. In order to fulfill my yearning for human contact while still abiding by the rules previously laid out for me by the medical specialist, I began serving as a nonmoving worker at a sporting-goods store owned by my neighbors Colby and Catherine. They welcomed the idea, because together they had no children, and I believe my young, fragile, pregnant self-created a window of opportunity for them to exercise their parental instincts.

Colby was not a tall man and had challenges with shedding pride, unlike my daddy. His excessive drinking masked a painful past of losing his first wife during childbirth. He barely functioned with his alcoholism, and if it were not for his second wife Catherine, surely he would have joined his first wife in death a long time ago. Catherine was patient and willing, and if they had decided to become parents together, she would have been a fine mother. Perhaps caring for Colby and the store kept her hands more than full. Despite Colby's tough, almost mean exterior, there was just enough "not mean" to amount to love for Catherine. I had learned by observing various couples that for some people, the lack of physical abandonment amounts to something worth speaking of honorably, even if the union lacks substantial emotion. Catherine loved up her husband with all she had. Sometimes I believe she was trying to wrestle away the demons from his first wife's tragedy so that the Colby of old, who was once full of life and full of sobriety, could reemerge.

I learned a lot about relationships and personal limitations through watching Catherine and Colby. There were similarities to my own parents, but Catherine was more stern than my momma, and Colby was less sweet than my daddy. And Colby yelled—a lot. The two met when they were much younger when she was a teacher and he a gym coach. She learned about his previous ordeal, but fell madly in love with him, and Colby, having since felt an extreme emotional block, could not deny that the spell was broken and that he, too, had fallen madly in love with her. The trauma Colby experienced after having had the two most important people disappear from his life in a matter of minutes compelled him to convince Catherine that they should not try to have children. She agreed, and later realized that no child born from her would be able to compete with Colby's increased grieving spells. He was both her child and her husband. In Catherine, Colby found a lifelong "help meat" and partner. And as one-sided as their relationship could have appeared to onlookers, I believed there had to be something that Colby also gave to Catherine in order for their marriage to maintain. In a different way but similar to my daddy, Colby needed more nurturing and support than his wife did. My momma's way of nurturing Daddy was by traveling all over the globe so he could spread the word of God. My daddy was the mouthpiece, but he spoke for both my momma and himself when he delivered messages. Colby might have required a lot, but it was he who provided the stability of their shared business so Catherine could maintain it and they could have a comfortable life. Through it all, they found a way to work together. Their two dogs, a poodle named King and a police dog named Damnit, were also a constant challenge, but somehow they made it work enough to turn a profit at their sporting-goods store.

I did miss my boys, but it felt good to be able to rub my growing belly in relative peace at home. When I returned home each day from the store, there was a lot of energy taken in to unload, and having animal talk with my furry friends proved to be a perfect way to decompress. Because I was alone most of the time, for the first time since I was a little girl I was able to truly talk to my animals. I returned to the days of staring into their eyes to feel a connection, or cuddling up to one or more for a time, which helped us all feel at ease. It was during these times that I began to reaffirm to myself my earlier feelings that I was being prepared for something greater. Was this the reason why I began hemorrhaging in a way that was not severe enough to harm the baby, but extreme enough to keep me seated most of the day throughout the remainder of my pregnancy? I have always believed that when God wants you to be still, a way will be made so that this happens. And your legs won't have to be broken to accomplish the goal.

My husband worked so much to keep up with me birthing babies. I don't know if he knew if he was coming or going. We obviously "connected" as husband and wife, but there was very little verbal communication going on. What had ruled our relationship from the moment we were married up until that point was a solid, unspoken understanding that I was the decision maker for how our life would flow. He had been on board for this since we began dating, and we were both in agreement with our family dynamics. My husband was a man of his word, and there was no doubt that he loved me, and he did whatever he could to keep my life as cushioned as possible. He dared not attempt to decipher my animal connection, and he also dared not attempt to stand in my way. In me he also had a solid, faithful "help meat," just as my momma taught me to be. And as my daddy taught me, I was also a determined, independent partner.

Baby Jama

Left: Ad for
Reverend Connor

Below: Early photo of
Momma and Daddy
(Rev. and Mrs. Connor)

Bottom: Revival
early days

Top: Early Connor family photo

Above: Jama with pup

Right: Jama, childhood school photo

Mexico

Jama, Little Lenny, and black dog

Jama and baby Charlie

IV

Noah's Ark Is Officially Born

Our third son, Nicholas, was only four days old when we arrived in Georgia, the state I knew would be our final residence. During my time of rest with Catherine and Colby in Indiana, I had a revelation that life was going to drastically change, and that sitting down during the final months of my pregnancy with Nicholas was supposed to help me become more focused on where my family's life was headed. Nicholas, though developed through a physically fragile time for me, could not have been in stronger shape as a newborn. At a full ten pounds, he was not a flimsy baby. Yet, I still treated him as delicately as I did when he was in vitro. As he grew, we barely allowed him to touch the floor, and we fed him everything in tiny, tiny bites, even when his teeth began to fill in. Because of this, Nicholas did not learn how to walk until he was nearly seventeen months old.

Around the time that Nicholas was close to six months old, my husband decided that he would schedule a vasectomy for himself, as he thought he could not handle one more baby. I panicked, because I knew our family would not be complete without that fourth child, who I deeply believed was supposed to be a girl.

As my luck would have it, we were ten dollars shy of the payment for the procedure, so the vasectomy procedure could not be done. Soon after, my brother offered my husband a job working alongside him for a trucking company that delivered Kodak supplies. I pressed to join them on their first drive, because at the time I was also ovulating. I maintained awareness of my temperature and knew exactly when the right time was to conceive. Nicholas was only six months old at then, but I was on a mission, and so I left him with Momma. The one opportunity I was given to cocreate our fourth and last baby together, I took. Within weeks of returning back home, I was pregnant again.

I asked Momma to break the news to my husband at church, knowing there was not much he could do with the news there. Just as he did with Steven, my husband cried. He later apologized to me profusely, feeling shame for not getting the vasectomy. He did not know that I helped orchestrate the pregnancy because God told me we had one more in us, and that that "one more" would be a girl.

We were so poor that I attended no doctor visits, I had no ultrasounds, and I took no prenatal vitamins. I used my previous three pregnancies as templates for what I should and should not do. Those memories and information helped a lot. I never felt uncomfortable during the pregnancy, and I was still able to help bring in money for the animals throughout my entire process. Being so busy made the time fly by. Nine months passed more like nine weeks. Soon I was walking as stiffly yet as quickly as I could out of the hospital elevator because my baby's head was popping out on its own. Within minutes of laying me on a table to deliver, our fourth child, a girl, was born. Her dad named her Louella Marie after my momma and me, and because the nurse commented on how "pretty as a peach" she was, "Peaches" became her nickname. When my husband held her for the first time, he shed a different kind of tear for his baby girl.

By the time Nicholas was off and running, we were living in our second small house in Georgia. The first house was literally a resting place to become settled near Momma and Daddy while the older boys were in school. The first small house provided an opportunity for my husband and I to gather our children and join again together as a family. Charlie and Steven were thrilled to have a baby brother, even if they were not allowed to fully engage in rough-and-tumble with him. Once my children were stabilized, I was able to zone in on our animals and be more conscious about the plan to grow what I began calling my backyard: "Noah's Ark."

We brought with us to Georgia three large dogs, adding to the two German Shepherds that traveled ahead with my parents when they took Charlie and Steven. We also added a family of cats, lots of birds, possums, squirrels, and chickens. Our second home was a bit larger, but we were still being squeezed out of it with the children and amount of animals. My husband was not home long enough to mind; he stayed busy outdoors while I steadily brought more of the outdoors inside of our home.

Daddy was busy building his church nearby, and because she knew he was going to return home every night from then on, Momma was more relaxed and had plenty of time to help me with my children. My entire family was settled and contented where we were. Even my husband became accustomed to walking in and out of a home that sounded more like a forest than the ones they manufacture at the zoo. He might not have had an affinity for animals the way I did, but I believe if he returned to an animal-free, quiet house one day, my husband would have been deeply affected just the same.

It is a wonder how I was able to concentrate with the various sounds in our house, from the spectrum of sounds from our children to the harmonic voices of several animal species. Yet, despite any utterances going on, God always made sure He was heard, and I made sure to communicate consistently. I always said a daily prayer and even a nightly prayer, verbalizing those things I had hoped for or giving gratitude for the things with which we had already been blessed. Prayer, for me, had always been as commonplace as brushing my teeth. I thanked and praised God all of the time. What I had never done, though, was perform a commanding prayer, which is a prayer that calls forth a blessing ahead of its existence. Through the noise and various voices in our home, God spoke to me as clear as day, telling me to command a prayer to establish more land for Noah's Ark because it was time to expand His vision.

I had no idea where the new land would be, yet I was sure it was in Georgia, because Georgia is where I was told my family's final destination on earth would be. Driving along the roads nearby, I spotted a house that rested central to what looked like over a dozen acres. There was no "For Sale" sign, but I learned that the owners attended our church. I approached them, and they were immediate in informing me that the property was actually twenty-five acres, but was not for sale, and that it was currently being rented to someone. This information did not discourage me or inspire me to look elsewhere, because there was no doubt that their farm was intended to be our home. Instinctively I knew I had to exercise patience.

For months I questioned them about the property to no avail. I was told and retold like they were broken records that the current occupants had no intentions of moving out. Still, I was persistent. Just as my journey had always been, all it took was one day to change everything. I could ask nine hundred ninety-nine times to receive the same response, but the thousandth time might be the catalyst for change. The wife always gave a sympathetic ear, and promised me that she would alert me as soon as the farm became available. I decided that I would pull back, but not pull out. I was going to ask every other month.

The twenty-five-acre land beckoned me to cultivate an enormous amount of patience. Their land was not filled with rolling hills and meadows, of which Georgia is rife, but it was expansive enough, and it was where God told me that Noah's Ark would have an opportunity to grow. After months of inquiries, it became very clear that the occupants were not intending to move any time soon. And despite my message from God, there was nothing physical to give me any sort of confidence that this was the route to go. My point of guidance was all spirit. In fact, all of the physical signs were telling me to search elsewhere. I asked myself a few times if perhaps I'd gotten God's message off. Maybe the *where* was not supposed to be specific, and I was supposed to focus more on the fact that we were set to move to a twenty-five-acre property, wherever that would or could be. Regardless of any passing thought, my spirit reminded me not to act on those thoughts and to remain focused on where God said we were supposed to be.

Like all prophecies I was given up until that day, I believed. I knew God was not going to steer me wrong. He led me to my husband; He told me how many children I would have, even assuring me the sex of our children; and He told me to gather the animals. He led me, just as I witnessed him lead my parents while growing up. I watched them never waver on their beliefs, and in some ways, I feel they were challenged more. When my daddy was leading us around the country and leading Momma in other parts of the world, his faith had to be ideal. There were no presiding parents or elders before him who could help strengthen his faith. He and Momma were all each other had for assurance and inspiration, outside of us children. For me, however, my momma and daddy served as the saving grace I needed in my adult life, and they never questioned my support and obedience to God. Their spirits only fortified my sense of belief, and I affirmed that it did not matter how long it took; I was determined to secure that land.

I depended upon my parents' support to help keep my patience strong, because just as quickly as I had convinced my husband that we were going to have the property, I had no timeframe for when the vision would unfold. Weeks turned into months, which quickly turned into years. The years that had gone by proved that God's idea of "soon to move" was calculated by a different measure of time. By the fifth year, my talking about the twenty-five-acre land had all but fallen on deaf ears. Still, I held my head high and continued to inquire about the property on my own. My husband and I would go about financially maintaining our small house with a yard, and I continued to care for animals the best way I could. I always believed that as long as I was doing all that I could, even if I was not doing what I believed I would ultimately do, I was still *doing*, and that alone carried weight. Regardless of lack of space and resources, I carried out what I believed was God's will.

Despite underlying pushback from my husband, I stuck to my guns and remained resolute about my decision about the twenty-five-acre farm. Most everyone was engrossed in the life we currently had, and my ranting about our impending "new home" made it sound as if I were daydreaming. While I went on about a life we would "soon" have, we also had to accept and embrace the life of actual struggle that we were living at the time. My husband did not take me seriously, and nor did the children. During the first few years, their emotions ranged from amazement and hope at my initial announcement, but in time transitioned to restlessness and annoyance because it was not happening. With the exception of Momma and Daddy, my family was tired of it.

Then, it happened. Though I had not lost my feeling for the twenty-five-acre farm, I had not spoken to the owners in about a month. It crossed my mind one afternoon, and just like that, she called me instead. "Jama, I know it's been some time, and your thrill might be gone about the farm, but it's available if you want it."

As if I had only been on hold a few days for the land, I enthusiastically responded, "Yes, yes we do!"

When I broke the news to everyone, it seemed like they, too, had developed a case of amnesia about how long we'd waited, because they were all elated just the same. My husband could hardly believe it. I could feel the tense energy evaporate from him when we arrived at our new twenty-five-acre abode. The children were thrilled, and after my parents watched all of this unfold, they praised God for what they already knew would happen. They were strong enough to hold onto faith for seemingly small things, like the possibility of their six-person family being able to sleep in a motel for a week, or for the favor of raising enough money so that we could eat. They were a solid team for God. In my household, though, I was the one who had to hold onto enough faith for two people, because I was one half of a different duo. My partnership with my husband consisted of me setting the tone that I was given from God, and because my husband's devotion was through me, he depended on me to always ensure that things would be okay. He looked me in my eyes soon after we arrived at the farm, sending me a message of gratitude for me not allowing my faith to wane.

The year was 1985, and we finally had our farm. As always, once he was on board, my husband was steadfast and diligent. Though the former tenants resided on their land six years, they left the farm in such poor shape, they might as well have lived there for decades without a maintenance plan. We were a bit stunned, but undeterred. The owners bought materials to fix up our new home, and my husband led the laboring process. Once we'd completed our makeshift renovations, we established a maintenance plan of our own so the farm would not transition back to the same state it was in when we found it. My husband worked many jobs to keep up the rent, and I'd soon taken to dumpster diving for groceries and other odd things we needed around the house. We would wait for a restaurant to close for the day and wrangle dinner for a night or two. We'd also wait behind Eckerd's and bring in everything from fabric to medicinal items. For our growing brood of animals, we'd find locations that provided food for them and dumpster dived after their store closed.

Over time, the twenty-five-acre farm became a bigger Noah's Ark, and we developed a reputation for rescuing animals. Our lot of animals grew from one hundred to nearly three hundred in less than two years. We expanded our species count and began housing llamas, monkeys, bonorongs, and all manner of species in between. Our money-earning process was very intricate, and though we were still struggling, we ran a relatively smooth ship. Even I began to feel settled.

I noted to myself that the process to get to our twenty-five-acre rented farm was hearty, but it was worth it. As the animals poured in, the children and I made way for them, creating handmade habitats for them on the property. My husband and I had become dumpster-diving pros and knew the tricks of that trade very well. We knew what days and times to be where, and we even had a manner in which we would load our car with what we collected.

One routine, unassuming evening, we were met with a surprise. Behind a Kroger I encountered a teenaged boy lying in a sleeping bag. There were no adults accompanying him, and so I knew he was on his own. When I asked him his age and why he was alone, he replied that he was seventeen years old, and after much dysfunction with his family, he decided to leave. He thought that he would have a better chance of making something of his life being homeless than he would living with his family. When he told me this, I did not get the notion that he wanted sympathy, rather, only to be respected for his decision. I would have never violated his wishes, but I could not help but offer him a legitimate place to lay his head at night.

We did not have much money, but Noah's Ark was an incredible blessing and I thought it ought to be shared with others in need, specifically animals and children. I'd taken in homeless teens in the past when we had smaller places to live, and we were able to help them come to a sense of understanding with their families and move on. My inclination to do so was inspired from the vivid memories I had about my experience in Mexico with the orphans there: the way the babies all crawled in my direction on the dirt floor, somehow knowing that I would embrace them; my time with the little girl who was around the same age as I was then, but whose life had already been devastated from being deliberately splashed with hot grease all over her face. As an eight-year-old girl, I wanted to take her and all of the parentless babies home with us. It was from that experience, and how deeply it affected me, that I knew saving animals would not be my only mission. Of the two, rescuing animals until I had my own family was not controversial. I could not take home orphaned babies or same-aged abused children even if I wanted to. Standing in the gap for neglected children was something that had to come at the appropriate time when I was of proper age.

So, I sat with the teenaged boy and we talked for a while, and then I made the offer. He was speechless. As much as he did not want sympathy, he also did not expect to be offered a place to sleep. "We don't have much, but we are an honest family," I told him. He looked into my eyes in a way to confirm my sincerity. From that day on, he continued to travel to Kroger for dumpster diving, but he did so with us, and when he collected supplies and food, he added it to the family bag. My husband and I were not yet foster parents, but I wanted to help deserving teens benefit from some level of stability while they pressed on in life.

I began collecting young people almost as fast as I collected animals in need. I could not believe how many children were living alone on the streets with no one to help guide them. We might have had twenty-five acres of land, but our home was not sizeable, and before long, my entire living room would be covered in sleeping bags with homeless teens humbly squeezed inside. Some would stay for a month, some a few months. We allowed them to stay for as long as they needed until they felt comfortable enough to return to their families or reside with another family via the foster-care system.

One thing was for sure: the larger the family, the better a situation can function. We housed many, many young people, and we also taught them survival skills by having them work on the farm. Those young people helped take care of chickens, cows, llamas, goats … you name it. Animals like exotic birds and monkeys were off limits for safety reasons, but we taught these teens how to prepare their food or clean up around their habitats. The results of these troubled teens being given daily responsibilities with the children was very special to witness. I watched otherwise irritable, misunderstood, and highly defensive teens grow a greater appreciation for life, as well as care for a life not their own. These experiences influenced empathy with them, too, on impressive levels, and the bonds created with the animals helped to temper and calm their restless spirits. A lot of the anger, angst, or anxiety I previously saw with some would literally disappear over time. I could see myself in those young people in the way they communicated with some of the animals with their eyes. Who knows what each communicated to the other, but just as it was with me when I would do the same as a child (and still do), there was no doubt that what was being exchanged between neglected animal and abandoned teen was pure love.

I woke up every day feeling a greater sense of pride for what was being accomplished. Animals were sent to me practically every week, and though we had not yet established ourselves as a nonprofit, somehow we were able to provide sufficient food and care for everyone. I knew that we were on our way. My husband and I continued to work odd jobs, not knowing that despite my efforts to clean houses, stack lumber, or whatever else we used to do to earn money, God would begin to flood my life with all that I had been wishing for as a child and more. There would come a day when my work would consist of only nurturing animals and children.

༄

When I think of children, naturally the immediate

images that come to mind are the ones I birthed, for being with them was the first opportunity I had to bestow limitless love on a child. Throughout our family's winding road, my children grew and thrived, and they knew they were loved. They also were taught that love is so great that it can span infinite miles and throughout an infinite number of God's creatures. There was never a time when any of my four birth children felt that they could not come to me with a concern, or could not have private time alone with me. There was never an issue too small that I would deny my children the attention they deserved. Their point of view, regardless of their age, mattered to me; the specifics of their well-being was important to me; and I would willingly lie down on train tracks for them. They also are the most compassionate beings I have ever known, because they somehow understood that my mission was to be a mother to them and to many others. They had a similar understanding that my siblings and I had all of those years traveling with our parents, who believed it was their calling to help save souls for God. We knew they were there for us without question, and we also understood that they had a special calling outside of our family unit. I am eternally grateful to my children for their selflessness with me, as I know my parents were grateful to me and my brothers and sister.

Because my children shared in our family mission, they were clear that everyone received equal stage time, and there were few times when they called extra attention to themselves trying to outshine anyone. I think they exercised their levels of commanding more attention to themselves earlier on, for the most part. From the moment he was born,

Charlie required me and only me nonstop for the first several months of his life. Because he was my firstborn, and because that premiere experience for me was filled with feelings of inadequateness, unrest, and nervousness, Charlie was the one who broke me in, teaching me the concept of giving up all for the sake of another human being's comfort. His infant self watched me try everything under the sun to please him, to calm his cries to no avail. He watched me cry when I was not successful, and allowed me to humble myself in the most powerful of ways. Ultimately it was simple music that did the trick, but because he knew that my first instinct would not be to consider a remedy outside of myself, he allowed me to show him how much I would push the limits for him using myself alone. He was able to witness and feel that his mother would go to the ends of the earth for him. I always will.

I believe the more children you are blessed with, the more opportunities you have to show love. I'd experienced so much anxiety during the first several weeks after Charlie was born, God gave me absolute favor during my second pregnancy. Steven was my reward for having remained dedicated to his older brother during my and Charlie's "mommy-and-baby hiccups." When Steven was born less than a year later, he felt no need to test me, only the desire to cuddle and coo. He rarely cried, and slept under my arm every single night. With him I was able to experience every early maternal instinct I had inside of me. He was a momma's boy whose smile spoke the words "I love you, Momma." He also somehow knew that though he had an older brother whom I loved greatly as well, there was enough love for him, too. I had zero challenges with Steven until he became a teenager, and by then, all of my children were born. I'd neared the status of "been there, done that," and so his turbulent teenage years did not overwhelm or devastate me. Steven waited to test me, and I thank him for that! He started out as an ultra rule-follower, and perhaps he was destined to experience adversity later in life to actually show him another path on which he could have gone. I am proud that he chose to return to the ways in which he was taught. Today, Steven has taken the baton from my father and serves as the pastor in our family.

Nicholas, whom I affectionately call "Nickel Pickle," felt my undying devotion while he was still in vitro. Before Nicholas was born, I was a busy person, always moving. Throughout my first two pregnancies, I worked, took care of house, and tended to animals with relative ease. I was not known to sit down, because I always felt there was more work to do and more animals to save. Yet only four months into my pregnancy with Nicholas, I experienced a vulnerability unlike any other, resulting in me literally having to sit down. I began to hemorrhage terribly, and I did not know if I was going to lose my baby. I prayed long and hard about the results of my test to confirm that Nicholas was still ok. After learning from a doctor that my baby was not affected by the bleeding, I could have returned back to my normal activities, but not knowing fully if this would put his life at risk. The results of the test were a blessing that came with a message: calm down. I listened to God, and in turn, God helped me along that very special journey with my third son. I learned a new level of love for an unborn child. Each parent awaiting the birth has only one concern: good health for the baby. After my own near deprivation, I know how transient a life can be. God only knows how grateful I am and will remain that I was shown favor and my Nickel Pickle is healthy AND happy. Glory BE.

My baby who I should have nicknamed "Ten Dollar" due to her being conceived because we lacked the last ten dollars to pay for a vasectomy procedure for my husband, waited well until she could speak full sentences to claim her moment. "I want to be in a beauty contest," my then three-year-old daughter, Peaches, told me, putting her hands on her hips, reminiscent of when I made my own grand statement about animals to my mother at four years old. Beauty pageantry was an industry of which I had zero knowledge, though. I knew about the fancy dresses and way too much makeup, but what it took to get there, I had no idea. Still, I told my little Peaches that we would help her compete. I can remember dumpster diving behind Eckerd's with a special purpose that evening. From there I'd found lots of little girly things for her in the past, for I loved to adorn my only little girl, but this time I was searching for the most frilly of frills to doll her up. I found bows as usual, but as luck would have it, I also found a spool of beautiful lace. I sewed lace trim on her dress and even on her socks (this detail she was most proud of), and we somehow paid the necessary fees for her to compete.

Standing on the stage with all of the little girls with lips so glossed they looked wet, and wearing enough eye shadow for a grown woman, I felt a bit uncomfortable for our little girl, who was beyond green about that lifestyle. She stood there with her beautiful, long blonde hair, a thousand-watt smile, and lost the competition. The baby Jama in her was not satisfied with the outcome, though, and she announced to the audience that she would have won if they'd paid more attention to the lace around her socks. My baby girl. To this day, Peaches is a strong force of nature. I have a great love and respect for her because of it.

When each of my children was conceived, God knew the love I had for them would have me traveling to the moon and back again. They know that they are my most valuable prizes, because every time I was able to give birth, a miracle of the greatest proportions occurred.

I am most grateful that my four birth children grew up knowing how much I love them, and they understand that the love I also have for Noah's Ark and all that comes with it has been transferred equally.

V

There Is No Credibility Better Than That Which Is God-Given

Most say living on love is not enough, but that is honestly what we were doing every day at Noah's Ark. We were able to function largely because of the support and love we had for our mission, and from the time-to-time love from common strangers who supported what we did. By the time we were close to celebrating our fifth anniversary on our twenty-five acres, our animal count had reached over three hundred.

Momma and Daddy were so proud, and so were we. My husband and I were getting along well, our birth children were happy, and we were able to support the teens who needed our assistance along the way. Everyone on the farm had specific jobs that made for a smooth system. Both indoors and outdoors were immaculate, and every animal was well cared for. I would stand in front of our home and marvel at all that had been created under God. Glory be.

On my feet in amazement one day in front of the farm, marveling at how far we'd come, several trucks and cars pulled up onto the property. I was aghast. While the occupants of the car fleet sat still in their vehicles, one man stepped out of his car and approached me.

"Are you Jama Hedgecoth?"

"Yes, yes I am. I'm Jama Connor Hedgecoth."

"Is this your animal sanctuary, Noah's Ark, where you house animals?"

Beginning to feel suspicious, I hesitated. I looked at the small sea of vehicles and felt the need to protect my animals and family. "Why do you ask?"

"I ask because if you are the Jama Hedgecoth who runs Noah's Ark Animal Sanctuary, I am here to tell you that you will have to cease operations, as you do not possess any of the necessary permits to house all of these animals." There were representatives from USDA all the way to the State Department with him. "This is extraordinary," he said. "We don't usually travel in packs like this, but because of what we've heard about how rapidly your establishment has been growing, you have landed on all of our radars at once. So we decided to pay you a visit."

Was I hearing correctly? Did he say that he wanted to close Noah's Ark? I could not believe it. After all that we'd been through, the sacrifices we'd made? I prayed long and hard for this place, and I believed this is where God wanted us to be. I did everything I believed I was supposed to do—except apply for proper credentials. I wished I had made that a priority while everything else was going on. But we were growing, and people were supporting us, and we were doing no harm. We were servants doing God's work. This could not be. I had to stop what was happening before me from happening.

"Can I show you around?" I asked the gentleman as calmly and confidently as I could.

"Well, sure ... Why not?" he said. I don't think he expected me to respond without being defensive.

I walked him and the other representatives around the farm and introduced them to all who was home. Though they were most likely trained to keep a poker face in situations like this, they could not help but comment about our grounds, surroundings, and how well kept the animals were.

Before long, the agent spokesperson expressed that they had to move along. He took a moment to speak with his fellow agent associates, and returned to tell me that each of them had no choice but to give me the necessary permits on the spot. They were not prepared for such a large amount of animals, and seeing how immaculate our farm was, they decided that it would be easier to allow the animals to remain where they were rather than try to relocate them all. They commended our facilities and gave us well wishes, encouraging us to grow.

And just like that, they were gone.

The unforeseen encounter with the agents began with me feeling an incredible level of stress. It was the first time someone had suggested the possibility of my animals being taken away from me. It is a vision I could never conceive, an idea I could never consider. My children and my animals are indeed God's children and belong to Him first, but they are also my life.

When those agents pulled up, I was in one of the most secure states of being I had ever been in. I felt resolute about where Noah's Ark had arrived, and I was clear about where we could go because I believed in the power of something greater than myself. That sense of faith is what brought us to where we were, and would continue to help us through.

Resting my head on the pillow that night, I could not drift off to sleep without hearing in my head the last word spoken to me by the agent. "Grow," he encouraged. We had grown. We'd become something that never in my wildest dreams I thought we would be, but I honestly did not have a scope of how big, how large we would grow, because I have always believed that the dream of Noah's Ark will happen and would be shared with no bounds or limitations. As I finally began to fall asleep that night, I thanked God again for the immense favor we'd been given in receiving all of the necessary accreditations to function as a legitimate animal sanctuary, all in one day. I believe that it all worked out due to me showing no wavering of my faith in Noah's Ark when the agents arrived. You'd be surprised at how much you can convince someone of your worth simply by believing in yourself.

The surprise visit from the agents brought forth more than the gifts they bestowed to us in the form of permits and accreditations. Soon after their departure, I began to envision an even greater possibility for Noah's Ark. Up until that time, I'd worked my hand as best as I could for that land and the growing number of occupants on it. My goal each morning was to rejoice in *that* day that the Lord hath given, not anticipate what would happen a year from then. Unless God put a feeling in the center of my heart, I moved day to day the way I believed God would have intended. Visions came from God and God only, and I spoke aloud the greatest vision when I was only four years old, knowing that I would one day have an animal sanctuary that would also be a haven for children. Those two bold visions I had in the center of my childhood heart had come true. What more could God dream for me?

An indescribable feeling struck me while I was feeding horses and overlooking the pasture over Labor Day weekend. It hit me in my chest like the wind had been knocked out of me, which made me pay even more attention.

I went to bed that Monday night hearing over and over again one very serious message: God wanted us to have more land. I tossed and turned, thinking God would eventually let the night be, but He did not. In the stillness of our bedroom, I experienced feelings of hope and anticipation so penetrating that all I wanted to do was pack up our entire house so we could be ready. So, on Tuesday morning, I began to do just that.

I moved in such a trancelike state that I neglected to formally consult with my husband. He walked into the living room and saw me folding clothes and packing them into boxes, and asked me what I was doing. I told him that we had to be ready. I told our children the same when they asked me. My husband acknowledged that this would mean giving up the twenty-five-acre farm we'd waited six years to secure after only having it for six years. I agreed with his observation, and then told him about my feelings and reminded him that we had to be ready.

From that day on, we lived out of boxes in our own home. The children asked if they could keep some clothing in their drawers, and I told them they could not, as if our impending departure could be as abrupt as fleeing a house fire. That kind of exit might not have been called for, but nonetheless, we had to be ready.

The reason why I immediately acted on the feeling I

received was because that level of conviction had entered my spirit only certain times before: when I laid eyes on my husband; when I was told by God that we were going to have four children, three boys and one girl; when I was told to keep my focus on the twenty-five-acre land; and the two early, pivotal childhood moments when I had visions of saving animals and children. We had settled in very well on the new land that became Noah's Ark, the land for which we'd all waited so patiently, and on which we'd saved the lives of and housed hundreds of animals, along with helping various homeless teens. Despite the daily struggles of raising money to pay bills, God always made a way. We had no humanly reason to want to leave this place that was fulfilling a dream. And if this inclination was some sort of "wish," I knew the difference between a human wish and a divine vision, and this was the latter.

My family, however, did not understand why we had to pack when we had no secure place to go. This third home in Georgia helped to put us on as solid ground as we had ever been. We still did not have much, but we learned various ways to earn money to keep our ship afloat. No one wanted to move. My husband commented as he stepped over boxes and bags placed centrally in our living room. The boys complained there was no room to play in the house. Peaches soon learned to be agitated just the same. But I persisted. Over the course of seventeen years of marriage, I realized that I was turning into my parents mixed in one: I'd been orchestrating frequent location changes for my family for a cause I believed in, just like my daddy. And like my momma, nearly as soon as one baby was born, I was set to deliver another one. And like the experience my parents set before me, my family was poor, and our livelihood was not secure. My husband was on board enough not to leave us, but unlike my parents' union, I felt growing tension in him brewing in our midst. I did my best to pretend that it did not exist, but there was only so much time that I could hold my breath.

My husband continued to question me for a plan. I confessed that I did not have a plan, but I knew that I would be given a sign once we came across the chosen location. I did not want to take any of our meager earnings to pay for extra gas to search for the next location, so we collected aluminum cans to cash in to fill up the gas tank. For as long as the gas would last, we'd pile our children in the car and drive up and down the dirt roads of South Georgia.

The state of Georgia further represented patience for us. After patiently waiting for six years for the twenty-five-acre farm, nine months of waiting and living out of boxes went by in a relative zip. Not long after we began our drive, I had an inkling. "Turn here," I instructed my husband as we crossed the interstate. As we drove right in front of it, cold chills ran over me. "Stooop!" I exclaimed as my husband slammed on the breaks. I stepped out of the car and onto the property, a vast, mostly unmarked expanse of land. There was a tiny "For Sale" sign that could easily be missed if one was not looking for it. "This is it. This is the land," I turned and yelled to my husband with confidence. I needed to walk further onto the land, and as I did, I disappeared in the tall grass that grew freely in the pasture. I ran all the way up the hill to some pecan trees and dug my hands in the soil. The rich dirt felt like it could nurture our Ark without end. In that moment, I heard a whisper in my ear. "Buy it," I was advised. I returned to the tiny sign, wrote down the contact information it provided, and ran back to the car.

"Did it say how much?" asked my husband.

"No, there wasn't a price," I answered, "but there was a phone number. Whatever the price, we will pay for it. God's gonna buy it."

My husband shook his head.

I called the phone number repeatedly to no avail. After multiple attempts to contact the realtor, she finally answered her phone, and I inquired about the acreage and price. "One hundred twenty-two acres for four hundred eighty-three THOUSAND dollars," she told me flatly. She then went on to talk about financing and real-estate talk, and because I did not seem like I comprehended what she was talking about, she quickly lost interest. I cut to the chase and told her that I'd pay the bill in full in one year. After that bold and peculiar declaration, she cut our conversation short. She was not convinced that I was a serious potential buyer.

I tried to contact the agent again the following day, and she ignored my requests. This led to me venturing downtown to find and hopefully speak to the owner. It did not take much time to locate his whereabouts.

When we pulled up to the owner's house, I said a prayer, hoping the actual owner of the property would take me more seriously than the realtor. I walked cautiously to the front door and knocked on it like I meant it, but not with too much enthusiasm. The owner's wife answered the door and advised me that he had recently been released from the hospital for a triple-bypass heart surgery. I mentioned that I wanted to talk to him about buying the property. She called for him immediately.

He walked feebly to the door and asked who I was. I gave him my full name, and he said that he'd heard about me, that I was the one with no money who promised to pay a half-million dollars in a year. He laughed. His wife smiled. I stood my ground and validated what he'd heard, going on to reiterate my offer. "Yes, I will pay off the bill in a year."

"How will you do that?" he asked matter-of-factly.

"Are you Christian?" I countered.

"I am," he confirmed.

"Then you know I can do it."

☙

On that next hot day in May the owner walked us around the property, and the more we walked, the more God's dream was made clear to me. The depth of the meadows, the not steep but lengthy hills—they were all part of the ultimate plan for what and where Noah's Ark would ultimately be. The owner had confided in me how special the land was to him, how much he loved it. *A loved land*, I mused to myself. *When Noah's Ark becomes officially founded here,* I thought, *it shall not be moved*. I had thanked him for his time, and we scheduled a time later in the week when we could reconnect. He would serve me the contract, and I would establish a payment plan.

When we arrived back home that night, I sat down with my husband and flushed out all of our current sources of income. With his various jobs and my little "Designer Pig" selling business, we could wrangle up about two thousand dollars per month. My daddy told me that he could secure a $10,000 donation, which would serve as a down payment. We could promise to do that for some months, knowing that these payments would not go toward the principal price of $483,000.

Our next meeting with the owner was direct. I told him about my plan and that he had to trust me on the rest. I agreed to close the official deal the following week when my daddy would have secured the $10,000 check.

I prayed long and hard prior to the deal-closing day. Before me was a sizeable undertaking, but I was not scared. God kept whispering in my ear, "Be strong, Jama. It is going to be fine."

The owner had a thick stack of bound papers in his hand that he handed to me. He advised that I have a lawyer look over the paperwork before I signed the contract, and gave a concerned comment about me not having one present with me that day. I told him that I was representing myself and did not need an attorney. He asked me how I would be able to comb through the contract to see if I had any questions. I asked him again if he was a Christian. He confirmed this truth a second time. I asked him if he was honest. He said yes. I asked him for a pen.

☙

We officially moved onto our new, blessed, *owned* land on June 1, 1990. I could not believe what surrounded me every morning. The residence was a bit shabby, but the land?

The land was majestic. It looked like one great, big, flat hand of God, and we would all be living in the center of it.

Our previous twenty-five-acre farm felt expansive, with plenty of room to create natural habitats for the animals. Likewise, this new property went on and on, giving us a palette unlike any other to work with. I embraced this new land as a unique opportunity to express through animals and children how we can all thrive together in harmony on earth.

The culture of Noah's Ark has never been about conformity; rather, the opposite. All differences are embraced. Everyone and everything has something to learn and teach. I have never encouraged any of my children—birth, foster, or adopted—that they had to like or do the same things as others. I appreciate the various talents and strengths of everyone. My singular requirement, though, is that they acknowledge that which is greater than ourselves, because I believe that it is from this that all of our blessings flow. I am but a mere steward, a conduit who does her best to listen and take heed to God's vision. And our differences work together to ensure that that vision manifests into reality.

Despite my willingness to always take heed in what God commands me to do, the small amount of wisdom I had cultivated during my thirty-two years on this earth kept me aware that adversity could and still would be a part of our initial experience. I believed I had a solid plan to come up with the $2,000 monthly payment. I'd chosen to pull from resources that had been previously proven to be tried and true. I was confident in our abilities to raise money from these sources, and I honestly thought that we'd end up pulling in more money than we expected to make the previous owner more than satisfied. But the outcome was the reverse. We failed at earning the agreed upon $2,000 every month, and every month we were also late when paying. After he walked me around what he considered to be his "special land" months before, I looked him in the eyes and, after questioning his level of honesty, I signed the contract without having an attorney present. He held up his end of the bargain by selling us the land. There were no gaping holes or other safety issues on the property, nothing that had created any concerns on our end. It was me, the one who approached the deal so confidently, who was falling short.

We were four months into this dreadful beginning that did not seem like it was coming to an end any time soon. By the fifth month we were really struggling, trying to make up previous balances not paid in full. By the six month, we were technically three full month's payment behind. The previous owner and his wife had been nothing but the epitome of grace throughout this process, but I knew in my heart they would have to do something to protect their interest.

In December of 1990, the *Atlanta Journal-Constitution* wrote a cover story featuring our beloved great horned owl, Humphrey Bogart, with the title "Noah's Ark Animal Farm, A Cloudy Future." This print story was followed by a local television news story, both of which felt like a blur because none of us understood the power of media at the time, and only cooperated with the interviewing process because both outlets promised to spread a good word about Noah's Ark. The positive word was indeed spread, and soon after the stories ran we had over seven hundred visitors from all over that donated for the animals. The turnout was overwhelming. I swear I ran around that land so many times, I am sure I covered a half-marathon's distance.

It is interesting that when people come to support Noah's Ark, sometimes they come to donate money or items to help our mission. Other times, folks think that bringing more animals our way is a good way to support us. It is true that we had not turned down an unwanted animal, yet if supporting our growth is not matched with actual supplies to feed our growing family, this can create an even greater need on our end. At Noah's Ark, we help, and we need help. It is a constantly moving wheel. I have come to understand and ride this wheel fairly well, yet moments of imbalance will always be in the horizon. It is our job as we grow stronger in our mission to be able to forecast these times, and be prepared when they come. One of my greatest dreams has been to be in a position of preparation, but until that time came, what called my focus most was the present.

When my mind was set mostly on praying that we would receive monetary support to keep our struggling ship afloat, there were the unexpected people whose outstretched hands instead passed along more animals who they believed would live better with us than anywhere else. And no matter what, these experiences are always mighty humbling. Someone once placed a badly injured bunny in my hands whose left ear was half cut off, and the other ear was covered with maggots. I wanted to cry for more than one reason. I did not deny the bunny, but I had no idea what I could do to help it. I wrapped up the bunny and carried it with me as I ran from one part of the Ark to the other, trying to provide it with a sense of tenderness, which was the best I could give it at the time. Engaging with supporters with sweat pouring down my temples, someone tapped me on the shoulder and asked if they could help. Immediately, I thought aloud without turning around, "Is there an animal you have to offer Noah's Ark?"

The response was no.

Then I turned around to see a kind-faced woman wearing pigtails. She looked sincere, and expressed genuine concern about the bunny in my arms. I told her that I appreciated her words, and I had been carrying the bunny hoping something would come to my mind and heart to help it, but without a proper veterinarian, I was at my wit's end about what could be done. I added my assumption that the bunny was also beyond her scope of troubleshooting. The woman reached for the injured bunny and said, "I will help. I am a veterinarian. My name is Karen Thomas."

I froze. For years we'd operated piecing together our vet support for the Ark through various doctors who would do this or that here and there, never having enough funds to fully staff a doctor to help our animals. Just like that, this kind-faced woman, Karen Thomas, filled that void at an incredibly unlikely time. That little bunny had served as the inspiration and saved the day for all of our animals and the hundreds that had yet to arrive. Karen Thomas, who we all soon began to call "Doc T.," became our angel veterinarian for Noah's Ark.

My parents sat underneath a tent to shade themselves from the scorching heat as supporters stood in line, giving donations to help us not sink. Each person was more benevolent than the last, and our gratitude for the presence of everyone was immeasurable. My encounter with the kind-faced, pigtailed veterinarian provided a boost that I sincerely needed, because later we learned that even the combined donation amount was still not enough to pull us out of debt or fully feed the animals. As overwhelming as the time was, I had to remain focused and keep my faith strong that God had something else brewing on our behalf. Doc T. served as a sign of this truth. She was our grace.

In the eye of any storm, I believe that God remains armed with grace to show us all that there is always a blessing in the midst. Sometimes the chosen act of grace (though always integral to the blessing) is so small that it can be overlooked. This is when people go through hard times not believing that God is with them. I believe He is always with us, no matter what. It is our job to see the grace during every trial and tribulation, because it is there. Overlooking grace leads to not receiving the blessings we all so desire. Regardless of how great a calamity, there is always, ALWAYS grace. Some people understand the grace message as "every cloud has a silver lining." The same here is true. If you cannot pinpoint a silver lining in any given moment or time of adversity, you cannot receive the gift that will help you grow and move forward. I not only have always known that grace is real, and that these silver linings exist—I depended upon them. And because I was so attentive, when a surprise animal donation came in from a gentleman named Henry F. McCamish, my antennae stood up.

He was pleasant, yet had a commanding voice. Through his serious tone, I could tell that he had an integral passion for animals. He told me that he'd seen our story on the news with his wife, and she was deeply moved by it. Almost strangely, he did not offer an open donation. Instead he asked me, "What is your dream animal for Noah's Ark?"

At that time of extreme financial deficit, a dream animal donation was far from an immediate need—or want. The concerns I had every single day during that time of deficit were how we would feed the animals we already had *and* still pay rent. I was not particularly looking to bring in more mouths to feed out of a sense of wanting. What we needed was money. But something told me to not derail the gentleman's interest. After all, everyone donates for a reason. Some people donate money as a tax write-off only, which, like those generous others who gave for the animals previously, could not have been his interest, because we had not yet accomplished 501(c)(3) status. Some people donate money because they want to help maintain programming, some donate in kind with food, supplies, or animals. Those who bring animals to Noah's Ark have a different connection to the place because they leave a mark through the animals they donate. Providing another living, breathing thing as a representation of one's self is a blessed thing.

I stopped thinking about how much money we needed and focused on Mr. McCamish's altruistic benevolence. "A dream animal for me would be an eagle," I said. "If I could ever come back as an animal, I would come back as an eagle. They fly the highest and can be considered as the most aware physical being. To me, they are powerful and majestic, and even when they die, they do it with strength and grace. Having two would be very meaningful."

"Two?"

"Yes, two … But the only extra thing is eagles have to live in special habitats. I know this because I've done lots of research on them, and after learning about what it takes to maintain a good lifestyle for them, I pulled back for now because it is expensive."

"Define expensive," he said.

"About fifteen thousand dollars."

"For two eagles?"

"Yes, sir."

"Okay," he said simply.

"Okay?" I questioned.

"Okay, you'll have your eagles."

I was stunned. We chatted for a few moments more, and he asked me to send him a list of more dreams that I had, and he also offered to name the eagles, which I eagerly welcomed. "Stars and Stripes," he told me. There was perhaps ten more minutes of talk, and then he was gone.

A check for $15,000 arrived the next day to pay for the corn crib. Then, I added two eagles to my license, which took some time. Our special eagles arrived later from a research center in Colorado. Stars and Stripes were absolutely regal, and were able to live out the rest of their lives blissfully and free of any experimental intrusions. Wow.

In the envelope with the payment for the corn crib was a note and a business card of an attorney. The note instructed me to call the phone number on the card if I thought I ever needed a lawyer. I appreciated the offer for the eagles, but looked at the attorney business card like it was a bad thing. "People who are in serious trouble need lawyers," I told Daddy.

"We owe some money, but we are not in serious trouble. We've still got animals coming in!" I tried to remain positive.

With each rescue I felt like I was a clothing tailor in high demand but with no fabric to sew the clothes. Animals were continuously being brought to Noah's Ark, but Noah's Ark was on very unstable ground.

Our financial instability wore on the previous owner for as long as he could take it before he served us with a final eviction notice. He knew of all the good we were doing at the Ark, but business was business. I was deeply saddened, but I understood.

With such heaviness on my heart, for the first time I did not feel so strong. I had endured numerous losses and triumphed an equal amount of gains throughout our journey to this point. Never did I feel tired. Not one day did I feel discouraged. Yet, saying my deepest prayer on my knees in our home, I received no guidance or answer. Suddenly, I needed air.

I drove our old red pickup truck (that only moved in reverse) up to the pecan trees, the place where I first went when I felt the message to buy the land. I returned to this place to talk to God. Bending down on my knees, my arms trembled as though a force was moving through me, instructing me to pray. Surrounded by those pecan trees, I closed my eyes and spoke my peace passionately and loudly:

"You told me to leave the last place for here, and I obeyed you! You told me what to do, and I did it... It seems that now you have changed your mind, and I am all right with that, but please tell me, please give me a sign, something to help guide me, Lord! These animals depend on you through me, and so do the children! I depend on you! Lord, please help me. God, please show me the way. I will pack up and move it all if it is your will. Just please, please show me the way!"

After saying this, my eyes naturally opened, because there was nothing more I could have said. No more tears would form, and an unfamiliar sense of calm overcame me.

Upon entering our home, my family all stood in the kitchen. Neither my children nor my husband spoke to me; somehow they knew to leave me be. It was my daddy who broke the silence.

"What'd He tell you?"

"Nothing," I answered humbly. "But it's odd. I feel better."

"That's how it goes," Daddy comforted me. "He's in motion right now, no doubt. He'll take care of it." He kissed me on my forehead and I felt like a little girl again, like after he'd affirm my "weird love for animals" as a God-given uniqueness to my older siblings many years ago. My daddy always, always believed in me.

Sitting down at the kitchen table to drink a glass of water, it occurred to me to pull out the business card for Mr. McCamish's lawyer. I did not know exactly why I was going to call his attorney, but I thought that maybe he could at least read the contract that I'd never read and find a loophole to afford us more time to raise the money to put us back on a positive balance.

I told the secretary that I was referred by Mr. McCamish, and she connected me directly to one of Mr. McCamish's attorneys, Steve Merlin. I explained to Steve why I was calling and he asked me to fax him the contract, saying he would get right back to me. I drove into town to fax the contract and returned home to that same glass of water at the kitchen table and waited.

About two hours later Steve called back, furious. He spoke to me like we'd known each other for years. His tone was familiar and disappointed.

"Why would you sign such a thing?"

"I don't know," I said. "He said he was honest."

"The contract is not NOT honest, but it is binding," he said. "You owe over four hundred THOUSAND dollars! And you have to pay it, or else!"

Or *else*. That stuck with me for a minute. When I thought of those two words, the only thing that came to mind was losing the animals. Where would I keep over four hundred animals? They'd be taken from me, one by one, two by two, in lots and groups, herds and bunches. They'd be relocated to different places with people who might or might not love them. They'd have to readjust to a different culture, which might affect their happiness. We at Noah's Ark knew the different quirks of each animal. I'd bottle-fed many of them until they were old enough to be on their own in a habitat. Some of them slept on the floor in my bedroom while they matured. They would be all gone. I could not believe that that should be the end. Loving and supporting animals and children was my calling. I knew this. I'd known this since I was a little girl. I could not believe what might be happening, and the Jama of old and new was not going to accept it, either.

"Okay, does the contract say anywhere that I can be given more time?" I asked. "I just need more time. An extension.

That is all I need."

"You don't need an extension, ma'am," he answered. "To raise over four hundred thousand dollars in less than three weeks, you need a miracle. If I were you, I would get on the phone with the previous owner and plead, plead, plead."

"Plead for what?"

"That he doesn't sue you for everything you are worth." He hung up.

I sat there with the phone still in my unsteady hand, and my daddy, my husband, Momma, and some of the children stood or sat nearby, waiting to hear what happened over the phone.

"I've got nothing else to tell you all." I wanted to cry.

Daddy and Momma walked over to me and put their hands on my shoulders and prayed. "It ain't over, baby," Daddy told me. I know he put in extra for that level of belief.

While we sat in the kitchen in relative silence, something else was going on in Steve Merlin's office:

Steve hung up with Jama Hedgecoth, almost annoyed about the phone call. He could not believe that she'd signed such a serious contract with no legal representation, and there was no attorney that he knew who would steer her to sign such a thing with no income. He stacked the contract together and pushed it to a far corner of his desk. He opened a file drawer and went on to prepare for the remainder of his scheduled appointments and calls.

Then, his direct line rang. It was Mr. McCamish.

"Yes, this is Steve."

"Steve! How's everything?"

"Going well, sir, going well. How is Mrs. McCamish?"

"She's fine," Hank said. "We're having a lovely time, thank you."

"Is there something you need from me, sir?"

"As a matter of fact, there is. I don't know why, but I have a strange feeling that something is not okay with one of the businesses. Is everything okay?"

"Why, yes, yes sir, all is well," Steve said. "I've received no calls of concern."

"Are you sure? My gut instincts are rarely off."

"Do you want me to double check with any company in particular, sir?"

"No ... I don't want anyone to panic about anything. Are you sure there is nothing awry where I am concerned?"

Steve thought for a minute. Mr. McCamish was a very deliberate man, not whimsical in the least. Steve knew there was validity to Hank's concern, but from where? Steve looked around his office, and his eyes led him to that far corner of his desk where he'd just shoved the very serious, unadvised contract signed by Jama Hedgecoth.

"Well, sir, it does not involve any of your official businesses, but do you remember the woman who you donated the eagles to who has the animal sanctuary in Locust Grove?" said Steve.

"Yes, Noah's Ark. Yes. What's the issue?"

"Well, sir, I've come to find out that she unwittingly signed a contract that holds her responsible for paying nearly a half-million dollars within a year's time. She is months behind on her agreed monthly payments, and the remaining balance is due in less than three weeks."

"I see," said Hank. "What did you tell her?"

"I told her that she should pray for mercy that the person

whom she owes the money to does not sue her for everything she is worth." There was a short silence on the phone—not a long one, but enough for Steve to make sure the call had not been dropped. "Mr. McCamish? Are you there?"

"Tell her I will pay the balance when I return. Call her now and tell her."

Steve was without words. He had been faithful to Hank McCamish for years, and always trusted his instincts and followed suit on whatever he was asked to do. Theirs was a rarely combative relationship.

"Will do, sir. Enjoy the remainder of your holiday. Please give my best to Mrs. McCamish."

Mr. McCamish hung up the phone.

For the first time since I hemorrhaged while pregnant with my third son, Nicholas, I felt a sense of anxiety. I drank one full glass of water, then another, and then another. I could not fully quench my thirst for some reason. It was as if a force was trying to keep me sitting in the kitchen. I was not supposed to move. Then, the phone rang. Almost fifteen minutes had passed since I spoke to Mr. McCamish's lawyer, the one who took the wind out of me to the point that I was both speechless and dehydrated. I could not take another blow over the phone, no matter who was on the other end. I asked someone else to pick it up. Just as I knew it, right after the call was answered, the phone was being handed to me anyway.

What I was told within the next few minutes made me feel faint. Then the sensation traveled to my bladder. I could not go on myself, but what I was told sure made me want to. After a few "uh huhs," "yes sirs," and one of the biggest "thank yous" I'd ever given, I hung up the phone.

Everyone who was there for the previous call was still in the kitchen, waiting for me to respond. They, too, could not take another let down, but more, they did not want to be left in the dark. I took a deep breath. "A miracle has happened. Somebody is going to buy the land for us. Noah's Ark has been saved."

VI

Blessings Amongst Blessings

Securing the land that became the official Noah's Ark through the McCamishes' extraordinary kindness freed my mind and created an even wider space in my heart. What began with Margaret McCamish's chance viewing of a lone televised segment on Noah's Ark when we were in desperate need of support turned into an incredible blessing. We now owned nearly a half mile of land on which to rescue and house our wildest animal dreams. And after Mr. McCamish's attorney also became counsel for Noah's Ark, we were able to secure nonprofit status, meaning increased donations and support from corporations. The year was 1991, almost exactly 365 days since I signed the contract with a man to rightfully acquire his precious land to share, and because of God's grace I was able to miraculously fulfill the payment timeline I initially promised. That entire previous year was more than a test.

God had been testing our will and patience for twenty years (or in my case, thirty) with animals, children, and various voids in our lives. No matter the level of adversity, we refused to deny the presence of grace. We had been living without running water and electricity at times; we found our food out of dumpsters behind restaurants and grocery stores; we worked any and every odd job one could think of; and the fact that we were legitimately impoverished did not discourage us from sharing the richness of our spirits with others. Times were very bleak, yet I saw the light. Daddy and Momma were there every step of the way, reinforcing what they'd taught me all of my life: there is a God. And we always believed that no matter what, God is good. Onlookers might have questioned how we carried on with so much joy while having so little, and how it was that I continued to welcome in animal after animal, injured or sick, and later, homeless teens who needed food and a decent place to sleep when food was scarce for my own family. I was able to do all of this because I truly believe that the more one gives, the more one will be given. And the more one is given, one can elevate his or her benevolence.

 I have never aspired to be a rich woman, I was not raised to be flashy, and have never wanted to live near a fancy avenue in a big city where I could buy the latest designer clothes and have people fawn all over me. If I ever prayed for any abundance, it has been for the opportunity to share my dream of helping animals and children all over the world. This is where my sense of wealth comes from. I know that money is important to have the freedom of choice and in securing a stable life. I know the difference between searching a garbage can for food and eating at a nice restaurant, or having the option of buying fresh produce from a grocery store. I know the difference between having the privilege of pushing a faucet and having water pour out, and walking to a faucet that is bone dry. I have called cheap motels my home, have slept on floors with a single blanket, and have worked very, very hard to have less than the basics in life. And just because I never had the level of financial position that can testify to the feeling of having better monetary choices does not mean that I could not identify how great it might feel to have better choices. But better choices or not, I will never lose a sense of the purpose of all of this.

I remain grateful despite all of life's adversities, and I know that my sense of belief has made it so we always made it through. Throughout my entire life, because of faith, hope, and grace, God's hand has been unchanged. He has always shined on us in some way. And all of my life has been a blessing, because all of it has led me to the NOW. If I had one fewer night of dumpster diving, one day of me wishing life would be any different than what it was, versus me praying out of gratitude for what we already had, regardless of how little, this would have made it so TODAY as it is now would not be. Every single day is an opportunity to grow in some way, and now we were able to show and prove in a way that we had never known.

Everything began to happen at once. It was as if our blessings had been brewing and simmering in an enormous pot, waiting to erupt on us, but not until we were on solid ground. I had a feeling our blessings for Noah's Ark were set to soon pour over, and that life was going to become more comfortable than I could ever have imagined. The McCamishes not only gifted us with the land, they supported us with a small staff to handle the proper care of the animals and immediately began building on the land, too.

They constructed a sixteen-bedroom home specifically for my family and for what Hank considered to be my big habits: animals and children. The McCamishes built offices and various habitats for the animals we had and for those that were pouring in like rain. With all of the added space, we rescued bears and horses, emus, llamas and tigers, and then some. Each animal was unique, even if with the naked eye it looked identical to another.

With our animal family swelling so plentifully, God decided that more children were needed to balance out those blessings. As word grew about our animal rescues, somehow we also attracted more young people who were without a home, as well. We welcomed in every single one, especially because now we had better places to sleep! My own children were moving along into their teens and into adulthood, and my oldest and right hand, Charlie was setting his sights on beginning a life of his own nearby. With Charlie at the threshold of the door of independent living, God saw fit to bless us with another incredible human being who would also help serve at the helm: a young, quiet, strong woman named Paula.

I was busy at work building habitats, loving on animals, and relishing God's favor when a call came through from someone eager to volunteer with us. With so much to do every minute of the day at that point, I was excited to welcome her in. She was soft spoken and had a gentle demeanor. Our sanctuary is robust with animals and lots of tough jobs to fill, but I was not deterred by her obvious vulnerability. There was strength in it. I could tell that she was a person of integrity, because she looked at me unhesitatingly in my eyes when she spoke. She presented herself to be a woman of conviction who had no insecurity about her journey in life. Within days of volunteering at Noah's Ark, I felt the true nature of her aura and instantly wanted to have her near all of the time. She was only nine years younger than I, but I felt a deep maternal connection to her, and she immediately returned acts of kinship to me.

Paula would create a personal regimen that consisted of reporting to her job when required and visiting Noah's Ark on her off days. When she volunteered at Noah's Ark, she spent most of her time helping teens work through their emotional issues, serving as an ear for those who needed to tell someone about the pain they'd endured. She was also wonderful with the animals, but there was something about how she related to the young people. It prompted me one day to ask her about her life and why she was so drawn to children. What I learned:

Paula was born unplanned from a union between two teenagers that was not filled with love. She lived next door to her paternal grandmother, the only person who represented stability and consistent love in her life. She was Paula's grace. Paula's parents' marriage was not a good one, and when she was very young, her mother learned that her father had been carrying on a relationship with a teenager. As a result, Paula's mother divorced her father. Paula's mother chose not to take her younger brother and her along. Rather, she left them with their father and moved away. Paula felt abandoned.

Paula was aware of her father's wrongdoings, and at times she feared for herself and for her childhood friends who came to visit, not knowing if he would be inappropriate with them or her. When not at school, Paula spent every waking moment in her grandmother's house next door, and though she did not denounce Paula's father's behavior, Paula's grandmother did her best to protect Paula from it. Times were very tough back then, and families were not accustomed to giving voice to child or woman victims, the trend being to quietly wipe away the tears of those affected while turning a blind eye to the perpetrator. Paula's grandmother followed suit with this manner of coping, but Paula did not resent her for it. Paula was like many children who were taught to consider this kind of support to be love. Paula did not deny her grandmother, but not seeing her stand up to her father and his ways that sparked her family's demise had a great effect on Paula's life. Paula was ten years old when her parents were divorced, and subsequently, beginning at ten years old, she began giving up a little bit every day.

Paula received her high school diploma, but she did not soar in education, though she once proved to be a very smart little girl. She was creative and loved to learn, but when a child does not feel fully supported, they cannot fully grow.

And because she had no positive template, Paula lived on and got married to someone who she should not have, just as her mother had done before her. Yet, Paula's ex-husband was not the same man as her father. He was just not right for Paula, and she did not know how to get out of the marriage. She felt deep sadness about this. Paula's grandmother raised her to believe in God, but they were not terribly religious. There were times when Paula prayed about her life, but she did not understand the power of prayer, and the idea that God could fulfill more than your dreams can ask for. She did not know that God could *brighten someone's life when the person least expected it. Paula's life all of a sudden became brighter by helping the young people at Noah's Ark. She feels honored to help give voice to their pains. Paula said that she enjoys helping teens move past their fears, and feels joy when she sees that twinkle in their eyes that they want to go on and grow. She feels they are all her.*

All of what she told me made me weep and also brought strength to my soul. Paula made me stand up taller. She was delivered to Noah's Ark at the exact right time. She told me that she'd always wanted to be a part of a loving family, and believed in her heart that one day she would be blessed in this way. I welcomed her into the Hedgecoth family.

The irony of her age versus my own will never be lost on me. By law, the only way that I could have adopted Paula, even if I'd known her when she was a teenager, was if she were ten years younger than me. The fact that she was nine years younger than me, only one year short of ten, was a sign to me that even if I wanted her to be a part of our family back then, it would not have been possible. Like me, Paula was supposed to endure all of those years so that she could give a poignant testimony, and so she could have wisdom to offer to all of the awaiting teens years later. I remain grateful that Paula joined with us—grateful that though I serve as her mother today, she is a woman whom I lovingly admire and who inspires me. She has given all of us so much, and children who have spent time at Noah's Ark since her arrival can also testify to her dedication.

Paula walked through our doors and did not look back on her previous life.

Years prior she had sat in a waiting room of a doctor's office thinking about nothing in particular as fleeting thoughts of wanting to end her marriage entered and exited her mind. Across from her sat my momma and an aide who drove her in our Noah's Ark van to her yearly physical. The van was parked outside, and Paula was grabbed by the message on our van that read "Bringing Children and Animals Together." The earlier thoughts in her mind dissipated, and she was drawn to the mission statement on the sign. But she did not allow that hunch about what she read on our van to pass by. It filled her heart enough to make her write down our number and call Noah's Ark until she connected with someone who would point her in the direction of how to help volunteer.

One afternoon together with Paula changed both her and me. We both knew she belonged at Noah's Ark. We both knew she would become integral to our mission. Paula believed she was doing the right thing by dedicating her time to help teens with whom she identified, not knowing where her contributions would lead. Seeing herself in them, she felt inspired each and every time a teen was uplifted and chose to do better. She did not know what the future held, but she believed in how bright it could be, and she was steadfast in the mission of Noah's Ark. Every day we bore witness to the blessings that Paula coming into our lives caused, and five years later, Paula's blessing took greatness to another level.

Sometimes, being in the right place at the right time can show its worth immediately, and sometimes, the enormity of the meaning of taking heed to God's calling takes time. I know this, because my life continues to serve as an ongoing testament. Five years of undying support for Noah's Ark brought forth a moment of closure for Paula that she never knew she needed. The fact that I was chosen to be the conduit makes Paula's introduction to Noah's Ark beyond poetic. It is indeed a miracle.

That afternoon, my husband and I sat with Paula talking about our pasts and how far we'd come. Paula mentioned the influence of her grandmother Laura Bray, and how if it were not for her, she would have never known consistent love. She went on to share details about her early childhood and how much her grandmother stood in the gap for her when her mother and father were not around. The details she spoke soon lost their volume in sound for me, because I could not move past the name of her grandmother: Laura Bray.

When Paula spoke her name, I remembered years before when my husband and I signed up to work odd jobs to make ends meet. One particular job required us to clean out foreclosed homes set to be renovated or torn down. Behind each home we formed piles of "throw away" items, and in the event that something could be of use to us, we placed in it a "take home" pile. The take-home pile was never plentiful, because by the time we arrived, many of the houses had been vacated for a while and any items inside were well worn or not useable anymore. But in one small, weathered home, I found a box of almost-intact keepsakes. Fingering through the items, I came across birthday cards, love notes to a child, photographs (mainly of a smiling little girl), photo albums, and various mementos scattered throughout. *This was special to somebody*, I thought. *This was a part of somebody's life.* I chose to take them home.

When my husband realized that I'd placed a box of a stranger's family mementos in our take-home pile, he was in disbelief. "Why," he asked, "would you bring home something that belonged to a stranger?"

I did not know what to say. "I just cannot bring myself to throw it away," I said. I brought the box home and stored it in our attic. This is where the box was stored and subsequently forgotten. That is, until years later, when Paula spoke the name Laura Bray. I remembered that that was the name I saw over and over again on the documents, photos, and notes. I asked Paula how her grandmother spelled her name. Then I asked my husband to go to the attic and retrieve the box.

Watching Paula pore through her grandmother's old keepsake box was incredible. I could not believe that God had brought Paula to us to help us on our mission, and that we were safely holding a vital piece of her past. That blessed moment had me convinced. It was as if her grandmother, who by then had passed away, helped to create the path years before to the family she knew would embrace Paula the way she deserved.

A couple of years after that moment, Paula had become an undeniable part of our family, but something was missing. We all loved Paula, and I considered her to be my daughter. Because she was no longer a teenager, the ten-year-older adoption requirement no longer applied. I told her that I wanted to officially adopt her so that she could carry the Hedgecoth name. In May of 1997, Paula Hanson became Paula Hedgecoth.

During the time of Paula's adoption, my husband and I

had become official foster parents, and the number of children we welcomed by then had swelled to nearly three hundred. I am proud to say that we saw many young people grow up and turn their lives around, and have watched children not become products of their previous environments when they moved into adulthood.

VII

How the BLT and New Babies Saved My Life

My childhood dreams were being fulfilled in a very big way. By 2001, Noah's Ark in Locust Grove, Georgia, had celebrated over a decade of service. To date, we had supported hundreds of foster children through our Noah's Ark group-housing efforts, housed over a thousand animals, and I had become a grandmother six times over. Everyone and everything was growing up and moving on. These were signs that something new and extraordinary was on its way.

On a common weekday before sending the children to school, I received a call from the Department of Natural Resources about a drug raid in Atlanta where lion, bear, and tiger cubs were found. I was asked if I was interested in accepting them at the Ark. We had already rescued several animals within these breeds, and so I had no reluctance at all. "Bring 'em by," I said.

When they arrived, they were the sweetest beings, yet I could not believe the conditions under which they were held. The tiger cub's nose was scratched raw from rubbing up against the small cage they were all raised in. The bear cub's harness had grown into its skin from the harness being too small over the growth of the bear. The lion cub was neutered, and we knew this meant that he would never grow a mane. I was so in shock when they were brought in, I held my hands to my mouth. And there was something extraordinary about them as a trio: Because they were raised in the same pin since they were less than two months old, they had developed alongside each other and treated one another as if they were from the same breed. They might as well have been three bears, or three tigers, or three lions. I watched them snuggle up under one another, each protecting his brother in their joint quest for survival. I knew they were predators, but I don't think they understood their differences, and so chose to let them live as a little family. They were scared and traumatized, and I believed the worst thing I could have done was separate them.

I immediately got Doc T. on the case, and she prepared to operate on the bear cub to surgically remove its imbedded harness. I held the paw of the baby bear when he was put to sleep prior to the surgery and whispered in his ear that it was going to be all right.

While they all healed, I kept them in my bedroom. I often slept on the floor with them and talked to them and prayed for their healthy recovery. It never occurred to me to separate them, because they seemed so comfortable being around one another. I was so moved by their resilience and the bond between the three, and watched them grow in love. We did not have quite enough funds to build a proper habitat for them as they matured, so we created a house in the backyard for them during the first year, and not once was there an aggressive streak shown toward any of us.

We affectionately named them Baloo, Leo, and Shere Khan from *The Jungle Book*, and nicknamed the trio "BLT" for short. Boy, did they live up to their names. Baloo and Shere Khan were playful and mischievous at times, while Leo remained more conservative and kept a watchful eye on all that was going on around them. After the first year we built a larger area for them in the yard, where they lived for another six years. They ran with our dogs, and even my oldest son, Charlie, spent a great deal of time with them in the yard playing around with them. Charlie would later comment that the only offense he was shown by the trio was made by Baloo, who chased him (especially for watermelon and cake) from time to time. The boys had an unusual kindness toward humans and other animals.

Margaret McCamish then came to our aid and funded a properly reinforced habitat for the BLT, complete with a large clubhouse, lots of land to roam and run on, and a creek specifically made for Baloo and Shere Khan. Their paradise was set. In time, word of mouth spread about our "miracle boys," and people would travel from around the world to see them.

They were our little (or big) trio for the seven full years that we kept them together near our home, and it was not until they were placed in a space where the public could see them that the criticisms began.

Experts from all around who'd heard about our BLT were quick to advise me to separate them "as soon as possible." These "experts," who had never heard of a bear, lion, and tiger being housed together anywhere on earth, immediately thought the worst. They suggested that by keeping them together, we were putting their lives in danger. "They are predators," they'd warn, "and one day, they will realize it, too." I knew what they were, but I also understood their extraordinary life as brothers. When I tried to explain this to the "experts," they downplayed that aspect. "You will see, and it will not be good." Now that the boys were farther away from me— meaning I had to drive a golf cart to see them vs. looking out into my backyard—I allowed the words of those who did not know our BLT to penetrate. This caused a sleepless night or two.

"I don't know … " I would tell my husband. "Maybe I should separate them." So I did.

Within hours of being separated, Baloo, Shere Khan, and Leo all became severely depressed. I watched their emotional states decline, yet I believed that I was saving their lives, as I'd been advised. They would soon return to what they really were and all would balance, I believed.

It did not.

The jovial, playful spirit that was Baloo resorted to being a melancholy lump on a log. Leo and Shere Khan simply sat still all day. No amount of attention from any of us would do. And the crying! I had to do something else. Three days had gone by, and I had had enough. I told Charlie and my husband that I was going to bring them back together, slowly, and see how they responded. They both agreed, having seen with their own eyes how the boys were all a depressed mess.

My heart beat fast when we lifted the gates and made them all accessible to one another again. Would they attack one another? Baloo was first to enter the main habitat. Shere

Khan and Leo were next. The two cats moved slowly toward Baloo, and I became frightened. With clenched teeth, I watched them face Baloo and right away headbutt him. I knew then that all was good. Almost instantly, they returned to their usual selves with one another, and they have been loving and protecting each other ever since. The public and the "experts" remain in awe. I cannot give any reason for this miracle of a relationship except "it is a God thing."

⁂

It seemed like miracles were happening all around us where the animals were concerned, but in my "people world," the devastating blows came one right after the other. First, Peaches and her new husband, Titus, were soon to fulfill their plans of moving to Alabama, taking with them my grandbaby Makayla. My husband and I loved all of our grandchildren, but because Makayla spent so much time with us, she was the apple of our eye. The anticipation of losing her presence surely did a number on me.

Then, during that same summer of 2002, we all had to come to terms with what had been building up: Daddy was suffering from full-blown dementia. Fortunately, this diagnosis did not affect his kind spirit, but it rendered him terribly forgetful. Also, the condition brought on uncontrollable dizzy spells that would result in him falling and blackening an eye, or worse. My daddy, the man who once wrestled demons out of grown men in the name of God, the one whose strength I witnessed physically, mentally, and spiritually all of my life, was becoming vulnerable in ways I could never imagine. My momma was devastated, but tried to take it in stride. I did the best I could, too, but I could not deny that everyday a little bit of my daddy was lost. Up until that time, my daddy served as my confidante and ultimate champion. Any inkling of a vision I had, he was the first to stand by it. My momma had also been a constant supporter, but Daddy served as the spokesperson. He'd stand up to the most obstinate of winds for me, and to think that he was losing his strength was challenging for me to fully accept. While I was becoming somewhat depressed about him, a third problem reared its head: my marriage was also falling apart.

Makayla leaving and Daddy's mental illness affected me greatly, but I realized that having them around was masking the fact that my marriage had been unraveling. My husband and I were a match made by my teenaged self, not understanding what it meant to be a wife and mother, but proud to serve and be obedient to those early messages God spoke to me. I had not calculated to marry my husband in the sense that I had ideas about us and how wonderful a life we would have. I had a feeling that I was going to have three boys and one girl with him, and so I set out to do just that. There were times when I had to orchestrate things, but it was never for self; I only wanted to fulfill the purpose that I'd been given by God. I did not think about what would happen after marriage. I lived for the next baby to be born and for the next animal to be saved.

Along this GREAT journey, my husband did not complain when I chose to lead our family in many eyes of many storms. He trusted me, and that trust is a reason why we made it various times before. Without his trust as a partner, all that has been accomplished today would not be. And he understood that this purpose of cultivating Noah's Ark was not about him or me. Our agreement on that understanding was solid and founded, and could not be questioned. While I loved and appreciated my husband for being a steady partner during those trying times along our journey, for not trying to deter me from what I believed was my calling, our marriage was an example of what could happen when the marriage itself is not the key priority.

My husband and I fought over the smallest, most trivial things. He did not want me to have friends, wear certain things, or comport myself in a certain way. Since I was the alpha in our relationship, he did not challenge foundational things, but he did take issue with lots of details. This, I realized in empathy, he may have needed to do in order to feel balanced within our household. He was not a loud man, so his bark was never heavy, but in time it was constant.

From the moment I began to feel withdrawn from our marriage, I mostly retreated inward, and of course shared with no one except my momma and daddy. The image of two people who wanted to make a difference in the lives of animals and children could not be tarnished. Children and animals were my priority, and I never wished for my personal life to be entangled by people judging our strained union and then reflecting that on Noah's Ark. Also, we were dedicated Christians, and so we had zero conversation about divorce.

But I was miserable, and my former go-to was my grandchild or father. When those two could no longer shield or blanket my pain, I began planting rosebushes, and lots of them. Before I knew it, I had planted nearly four hundred rosebushes. To avoid talking to my husband, I kept busy outdoors. I preened and clipped my sorrows away, and when I completed that task for the day, I'd hang out in the kitchen with my parents or spend quality time with the animals. Daddy used to counsel us, which acted as a great big Band-Aid, but as Daddy's condition deteriorated, our discussions grew slim. Momma exercised patience with us and stepped in when Daddy could not, yet her fresh perspective did not give either my husband or me a different one.

There were many, many days, especially after Makayla moved away, that I felt trapped in the silence of my mind or the loud thumping of my beating heart. With no one left to talk to, I, Jama, for the first time, felt like a floating island roaming aimlessly in the sea of Noah's Ark. I have always enjoyed communicating with the animals, and by then I had almost thirteen hundred from which to choose! But I craved human attention. Our dysfunction made it so my husband could not offer that to me.

Peaches was the last to move away, for all of her brothers had grown up and created their own lives. Charlie was nearby, but had his own share of new family responsibilities, and I greatly respected that. He was so helpful with the animals, and did his best to stand in the gap for me. Paula continued to be the gift that she was when she walked into our lives. And while I could be her ear in full, I would never have expected that level of anchoring from her.

With how my life looked on the outside, some would think that I should have been standing triumphant. All of my birth children had grown up and moved on in ways that did not keep me up at night; Noah's Ark continued to expand; the animals and foster children were happy; and although my daddy was going down, I watched that man live a full life in service to God, and so I knew that when his time came, the bells would ring and God would welcome him with open arms. I did not fear for his soul, and I was raised to be selfless enough to not question God whenever the decision was made to take Daddy home. It was the status of my own life that had me concerned.

Each night and every morning when I made my prayers, I always made my peace with God. I have clarity within myself that despite those things I might have allowed to be initiated by my mind, I would be fine whenever my time came because I would know that whatever I had completed up until the moment God calls me home would be all that I should have accomplished in this life. Yet I now found myself making a different "peace." My sadness about the culmination of everything, mainly my marriage, compelled me to ask God to take me sooner than might be deemed. I did not feel equipped to handle all that would come after everyone found out that my marriage was failing. All I could see were the faces of friends, family, and supporters of Noah's Ark pointing in judgment. And those fingers were not pointed at my husband—they were pointed at me, the decided leader of our duo.

My husband refused to participate in outside counseling, and so we decided that we would move forward living together, although somewhat separately. I chose to go through the motions every day at home, but I began to feel like it was not only Daddy who was slowly fading away.

But God, as I have always believed, is a merciful God, and

wants only what is best for us. Sometimes we have to find ourselves fading away before something jolts our beings to remind us of our essence and give us the drive and strength to go on.

During that sad summer of 2002, I was called to nurture and aid two more babies. This time, however, the babies were human, and this was the very first time I'd been contacted about someone so young through foster care. A part of me was a bit stunned at this call, because, after all, we at Noah's Ark were accustomed to caring for at-risk older children and teenagers, not babies. Emotionally, I felt exhausted, and in my mind I could not find any logical reason why I should engage a vulnerable soul when my own soul felt so depleted. *But*, I reminded myself, sighing as the caseworker began to explain the stories of the newborns, *God always gives us what we need.*

Both babies were literally a few days old, unrelated, and had been left at the hospital when their mothers were discharged after giving birth to them. I'd not had a baby in my care in a number of years, and the idea of it all was surprising. Despite all that was going on with me, I was not surprised by my response to the task.

I arrived at the hospital with open arms. When I approached each baby, I was told that one was a very fragile case, having been born legally blind with a hearing condition and cerebral palsy. His diaper was soiled, and when I attempted to change it, sores from a previous diaper rash began to peel away with the diaper. Horrified, I rubbed lots of Vaseline in his diaper to help ease the diaper fabric away from his delicate skin over time. When I brought the two beautiful baby boys home, I sat them in their bassinets and looked at them. They were so innocent and perfect, despite the warnings I was given by the hospital staff about one of them.

Paula met me at the door to receive the boys. When she saw the look in my eyes, she hugged me and reminded me that it was going to be okay. My husband was shocked that I brought the babies home, but I paid him no mind. I instead focused my energy on bathing them and loving them up every day. I knew that in time, my husband would become attached, too. One of the babies was already given a name, Antonio, by his birth mother, while the other boy came to us nameless. Talking to Margaret McCamish one day following the boys' arrival, she had a revelation to call him Elijah after the biblical prophet.

The babies grew healthily as the weeks passed, and we as a family grew more attached to them. At the same time, my husband and I became less attached to what was going on between the two of us. My distraction was the constant development of the babies. Elijah, the baby with health concerns, began to experience miracle after miracle. It was as if these miraculous moments were sent as reminders of how God can turn things around. The reminders did not feel relative to my dysfunctional union with my husband, but to me as an individual. With each miracle I witnessed, I felt a little bit of light illuminate within me. First, his rapid eye movement, which caused the diagnosis of him being legally blind, began to steady after his first month. By four months old, he commenced hearing sounds again, too. We exercised his muscles daily, wiggled his little toes and fingers, and engaged him throughout the day to help keep his eyes, ears, and mind alert.

Antonio did not require this level of engagement, but we also took special care of him. We were so busy raising the boys that it did not occur to me that it had been months since we had heard from the case worker. After the fifth month, someone called to tell us that Antonio's grandmother was sending for him. I was heartbroken. I knew that they were foster babies, not set to live with us forever, but because I had not been working with a case manager for either of them, I easily lost touch with our actual situation. I allowed myself to love them as if my home was going to be their forever home. Then, just like that, Antonio was gone.

Now reminded of the reality that the babies would in fact be leaving, I nervously awaited the call for someone to take Elijah. Because I cared for him so deeply, our bond grew stronger with each and every milestone he achieved. For me, the separation from Elijah would be that much more difficult. A short time after Antonio's departure, a call did come. My heart felt like it was going to explode.

The caseworker suggested something that I had never been able to do with any of our foster children, regardless of how much we'd grown to love them: adoption. I could not believe it. *They are not going to take him from me*, I thought. My heart ceased pounding a mile a minute when I heard the possibility. It was true that I, a director of a group home, could not officially adopt a foster child. However, because he was a newborn, coupled with a few other reasons that made him exempt from this rule, Elijah became my first adopted son. This gift could not have arrived at a more perfect time in my life. God always knows what we need.

With Elijah's level of adapting and learning, I was unafraid of his diagnosis of cerebral palsy. I believed that Elijah's sight and hearing recovery were proof that he could overcome anything. And he did. We all continued to work with him, and before we knew it, he was talking. When Elijah achieved the walking milestone at sixteen months old, I was overjoyed. Since then, it has only been one proud moment after another.

I was not the only one who felt proud about Elijah's arrival. That first year and a half of Elijah's life served to help illuminate my daddy's final days. Daddy could not communicate as well as he once did, but he did laugh more. Before Elijah arrived, Daddy was suffering from feelings of being unproductive. He did not say this directly to us, but Momma and I knew that it was because he could not keep busy in the manner to which he was accustomed that he ceased standing as tall. Plus, his countenance alone spoke volumes. He could not drive, he could not pick up produce as he loved to do, and he could not help Momma around the house. But when Elijah arrived, Daddy could sit and hold him while watching us do all of these things, and knowing that he was responsible for this small baby put a smile on Daddy's face.

During those days of downturn for Daddy, Elijah was more than a saving grace for everyone. It was clear that Daddy's physical abilities were being compromised as time went on, but his spirit never waned. On the rare days when he felt more physically upbeat, he would tell me to get ready for church. He'd dress himself in a three-piece suit and stand by the door, waiting for me to drive us both to church. Then there were the days when I would pile in the bed with him and some of the grandchildren and eat ice cream and watch TV.

"Getting ready to go home?" I asked him one night, cuddled under his arm. "I've got this feeling."

He looked down into my eyes and told me no. The very next morning, Momma told me he was gone.

A couple of interesting things occurred with certain animals when Daddy was called home to glory. For one, our cat Tiger climbed into the hearse that carried Daddy's body and would not leave until Charlie crawled in and pulled him out. Then, as the hearse drove away, an unusually skinny deer came to Momma and Daddy's house. It stood there for a while before vanishing. When the skinny deer returned the next day, we fed it, and then every day it paid a visit to Momma and Daddy's house to be fed until it got fat. I suppose after it received the nourishment it craved, it decided that it was strong enough to move on in the world on its own. We did not see the deer again. As the deer created somewhat of a pattern about its food-replenishing schedule with us, I was immediately brought back to the essence of who Daddy really was: a man who dedicated his life to helping people replenish a sense of strength, well-being, and a solid faith system in God. He understood that even if someone had a buried passion to live their life for God, sometimes the frailty of a person's will might leave them less empowered to act on that inner passion. During my entire life, I witnessed the brilliance of how my daddy would gently, sometimes fervently, help people feel full of the word of God. He would fatten them up with scripture and guidance. After they were filled, just as the deer had done, they would motivate on their own.

Whenever I think of that deer, I am brought back to the

great conduit my daddy served as for God. He nurtured and fed thousands of people—too many to count—and those people went on to nourish their respective communities. I am proud to say that my daddy's influence through God has spread far and wide.

Momma said she missed Daddy like air. She soon became lonely and a bit sullen, but vowed not to allow those feelings to persist. One not especially extraordinary day, Momma rose up and picked up Daddy's workload. She took over buying produce, peeling potatoes—any and every thing that Daddy did around the house. She said that it made her feel closer to Daddy. She also appreciated that more things to do kept her even busier. "Busy is better," she'd often say.

For me, on the other hand, there was not enough busy to shroud what was going on in my marriage. Elijah was still very young when Daddy died, but he was soon on his way to talking after having recently learned how to walk. Toddlers can be a handful, but the minute-by-minute care that Elijah once needed from me began to change. He was learning how to be independent in certain ways, and thus I had more time to think about my declining marriage. I did all that I could to push any feelings of defeat way down, but I could not deny what was right in front of my face. I knew that any negative attention directed at my dysfunction with my husband would surely distract the continual good that was happening for Noah's Ark. I did not lie to my husband or to myself about what I believed was our reality, and thankfully, he did not lie to me either. Yet, despite what we both knew, neither of us attempted to sever our marital bond. There was a lot on the table, and my contribution to the delay was not because I was without belief that I could handle Noah's Ark on my own if need be. God beckoned me to remain in the marriage because there was something greater at stake, something vital that would require my husband and me to once again sign on the dotted line as husband and wife.

Above: Jama's birth children: Charlie, Steven, Nicholas, and Peaches

Right: Peaches at the child pageant

Jama mowing the lawn in Locust Grove

Parrot and monkey friends

Jama nursing a small horse, early days of Noah's Ark

Daddy (Reverend Connor) feeding a fawn at the Gravitt farm

Habitats in the winter

Margaret and Henry McCamish

Jama with Henry McCamish

THE McCAMISH GROUP, L.P.

December 13, 1995

Ms. Jama Hedgecoth
Noah's Ark Rehabilitation Center, Inc.
712 Locust Grove Road
Locust Grove, GA 30248

Dear Jama:

Noah's Ark has to be one of the "10 Best Kept Secrets" in the world of 501(c)(3) organizations.

Although you have shown significant growth over the past five years, you are still relatively small when measured by mere size, but certainly a giant when measured by what you have accomplished in the lives of those whom you have helped.

It's been and continues to be a blessing to Margaret and me to share a little of your dream. I know it's heartbreaking to you and everyone involved at Noah's Ark to have to say "no" to a child who so desperately needs the unconditional love and caring you so unselfishly give. I pray that others will become involved in providing the financial support that will make more of your dreams come true. They will never make any investment in the lives of others that will produce any greater return than an investment in Noah's Ark.

If anyone cares to do so, please ask them to call me at 404/261-4418 (office) or 404/841-1069 (home). I would love to talk with them and answer any questions they care to ask.

Don't ever give up on your dream to help others. The world needs more Noah's Arks.

Cordially yours,

Henry F. McCamish, Jr.

HFMjr/gw

Daddy (Reverend Connor) with a designer pig

Momma and Daddy (Reverend and Mrs. Connor) holding a turkey

Paula

Above: Noah's Ark sign

Right: Jama's son and right arm, Charlie

Left: Jama feeding baby Shere Khan

Below: Doc T, Charlie, while baby Baloo has surgery

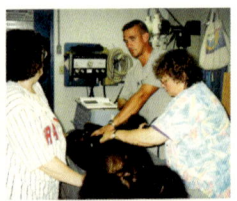

Henry McCamish with baby Baloo

Shere Khan with a puppy and piglet

On page 126: The BLT all grown up

Jama's grandchildren with Shere Khan

Jama with Baloo

Jama and Leo

VIII

A New Beginning

"Momma, I want a Dora baby. Like this one." Elijah reached up and showed me a photo of an Asian girl. He pointed at her face to bring emphasis to his request. "A *Dora* baby!"

I glanced down at my three-year-old son so eager to declare this request. "Baby, she's so cute, but Dora is Mexican. This little girl is Asian," I said. "I know she has the same hairstyle as the girl in the photo."

"Dora! Dora!" Elijah repeated. He was adamant. I brought my son along with me to Berean Bible Bookstore on Cleveland Avenue, looking for nothing in particular, but Elijah had found something very specific. I took the pamphlet he handed me and put it in my small purse and picked him up.

"You want a Dora baby, do you?"

"I want a Dora baby, Momma." In his eyes I could see past his three-year-old innocence to a clear, purposeful request. I had to stop for a moment while holding him and communicate with him through our eyes. I remember it being a particularly intimate moment that served as a turning point of

Elijah growing past toddlerhood. I had already raised four birth children (and had had a hand in raising hundreds more foster children), and so for me, though not birthed through me, Elijah was my sixth child, including Paula. Despite having five siblings, he lived as a single child because his older brothers and sisters were all adult age. He was growing up alone, and for the first time, I paid real attention to that.

☙

Because it was the last thing I grabbed on my way out of the door, my hand was firm on that same small purse I carried the day before to Berean's as I sat in the passenger seat with my husband on our way to the Piedmont Driving Club. The owners of a local company who were also board members of ours helped to host a Noah's Ark holiday fundraiser, along with longtime Noah's Ark supporter and friend Susan LeCraw and others. My husband and I were in Noah's Ark mode, so I did not expect real tension during our drive. He quietly complained about not wanting to attend, not wanting to be around so many people, but overall, he acquiesced to what I thought was best: him being present. And while I thought the Ark would serve as the focal point of energy for our drive to the Piedmont Driving Club, we somehow found ourselves engaged in petty arguing. I ended the back and forth miles before we reached the location, because I wanted my husband and I to be able to experience what was soon to present itself.

When we arrived, I had to take a moment to take in all that we were seeing. The holiday décor was breathtaking.

The building was elaborate with streams of holly and wreaths that sheathed doors and banisters, all exemplifying the spirit of Christmas. We were greeted by well-dressed men who held out their hands to escort us out of our car and then park it for us. For this big fundraiser, I was sure to have my husband to wear a suit. I wore a floor-length sparkly beige number that I'd recently bought at JC Penny, and I wore my hair in a bun. We were on the early side of arrivals, so I was able to walk around the quiet ballroom that was also beautifully decorated and adorned with various wooden animal carvings. I could not believe that it was all especially put together to benefit my childhood dream of protecting animals and children, which became Noah's Ark. My heart beat fast in anticipation of all the upscale people who would soon fill the room.

To my surprise, I did rather well communicating, realizing that speaking about something near and dear to me wasn't daunting at all. In fact, I relished it. When it was time for me to give a speech in front of the room, though shy at first, I soon eased into comfort to share some of my experiences that offered insight about my lifelong passion and love for children and animals. I never felt like I had to sell what Noah's Ark was. All I had to do was tell the truth about it, and people would embrace it. If they took the time to visit, there was no question how connected they would become. I have been around people who considered themselves "lukewarm" about animals turn to bona fide four-legged lovers after leaving Noah's Ark for the first time. I could not believe how well my words were received. Feelings of joy and elation overcame me so much that I needed some air.

When I made my way to an outdoor terrace after engaging in at least ten mini conversations along the way, I encountered those same hosts and spirited supporters of Noah's Ark. They were a lovely couple who did so much for our children and children in other parts of the world. They were happy to support us, and really were a key part of the candelabra of integral support created by the McCamishes to anchor our efforts. The support from this couple was foundational and fundamental.

I thought the husband would get right into the success of the evening and how the children and animals would benefit, but instead he brought up the possibility of adding onto our family brood. "Have you ever considered adopting an Asian baby?"

I was thrown. *An Asian baby? Where did that come from?*

"Cannot say I have," I replied. "You know, we are doing the best we can with the family we have now … " Then, it hit me like a ton of mulch. *The Dora baby.*

His wife interjected, stating that they'd helped a friend of theirs adopt children from China. She assured me that they'd be instrumental for me, too. By this point, Elijah's Dora baby would not leave my mind and heart. Yes, we did want a Dora baby.

"It's funny you should mention it, because just yesterday my son Elijah asked me for a Dora baby," I said. "He was pointing at a pamphlet about Chinese children. That same pamphlet is in my purse." I said this all while reaching down to my small pocketbook to pull out the brochure.

"Ever heard of the Great Wall Adoption Agency?" the husband added strongly. "Do you want a Chinese baby?"

"Yes, I do," I responded, still clutching the pamphlet and reminiscing about Elijah and his sincere yearn for a Dora baby. I could not believe this twist of fate.

"Then it's settled. You'll adopt twins."

༄

When I told my husband about my experience with the couple, he was not as keen about the offer. "How will we support a set of twins from China?"

"The same way we have supported all of our American children," I said. "With food and love." My husband was not pleased and continued to reject the idea, but Elijah deserved to have a sibling his age, and I was not yet full from motherhood. "We're adopting the babies, and if you don't like it, you can leave." I could not believe I spoke those words. My husband sensed the sincerity in my eyes. He relented and agreed to adopt with me.

Our supporters were true to their word and financed the entire endeavor. I had called the husband the following Monday to be sure that he and his wife's seemingly spur-of-the-moment offer was still good. His immediate response: "Go for it, girl."

The process was rather complicated and long. Along with funds from the supportive couple, we had to send over individual and family photos in order to be matched with children. It was particularly important for the photos to be clear because we would be matched with the children according to our eyes. When I told Elijah, who had just turned four years old, that we were going to adopt a sister for him, he could barely contain himself. "How long will it take?" he questioned daily. I practically stood vigil by the mailbox, hoping that a photograph of our twins would arrive.

For some, miracles can be instantaneous, but for me, everything of some importance in my life had made me wait. It took a little over thirteen months since we first sent photos for us to receive real correspondence with the adoption agency. When we did, we were greatly surprised. Though we were approved for twins, we were sent a photo of a single baby girl. We could have declined and waited for twins to be born, but something in me knew it was time and she was the one.

To celebrate our journey to China, the couple flew Elijah, my husband, my granddaughter Lauren, and me first class. It was a beautiful ride, and all the way there I could not get my new baby girl off of my mind.

Once we arrived and were settled in, we traveled to the orphanage. We stood in an oversized room with thirteen couples all waiting to meet their child or children. While we stood at one end of the room, there were nannies and translators who stood on the other side of the room with the snow-coat-wearing, bare-bottomed babies. To my eyes, they all looked the same, but Elijah spotted a wobbly little baby girl wearing a yellow snow coat. Within moments, she pitter-pattered over to my husband and offered him a tiny piece of lint she picked up off the ground. He tried to maintain a neutral facial expression so as to not overly engage himself or the tiny little girl, but he was visibly moved. A translator caught wind of what the baby had done, and swooped over to prevent her from being so close to the families on her own.

The woman's swift action startled us all, and the baby was returned to the group.

When our name was called, we stepped forward and a nanny walked over with our daughter. Lo and behold, she was the one who'd previously made herself acquainted with my husband, the one who Elijah knew was his little sister form the start. When I placed her in my arms, she did not cry at first, but upon hearing the wails of the babies who were also set to be separated from the group, she cried, too. Elijah patted her on the back and she calmed down.

I gave her a biblical name, Sarah, and it was most fitting. She was a knowing and poised baby, and all I could think about was how powerful she already was. But when we landed back home, Sarah displayed behavior that concerned me. Her extreme aversion to car seats was alarming. Several times I had to pull over on the side of the road to calm her down. Upon doing some research, I learned that the babies spent hours strapped down to potty chairs and beds. I was mortified, but I had to obey the laws and keep her strapped in a car seat when we traveled by car. And because I'd become so innately in tune with Sarah in a short period of time, until she calmed and became used to her car seat, I kept Sarah's car rides very short.

☙

Having to temper myself for a child—or even an animal that lacks reason—has never posed a challenge. However, when I am required to exercise that same level of patience for an adult, I find it difficult to understand the need for kid gloves. All while I was raising Sarah and Elijah, helping them to weather toddlerhood and childhood, I also had to express untold amounts of empathy for my husband of nearly thirty-five years while he trudged along in our marriage as my time and attention continuously had to be shared. Elijah and Sarah were blessings to our family, and inside, my husband loved them, but they still represented two more people who relied on me, thus making less time for him. And that was not a wonderful thing.

Along with Elijah and Sarah, we also had roughly sixteen foster children living in our home at this time. Though he initially agreed to everything, the weight of it all began to weigh on my husband. As my irritation about his constant disgruntled behavior grew, it occurred to me that if I wanted to give my marriage any real shot, I needed to find a way to empathize with him, to find a common ground of understanding.

It certainly was not as if I did not know who I married. I think I did not fully consider that this level of tension could grow in him. My husband was a simple man, and I was clear on this since the first time I laid eyes on him when I was fourteen years old. He wanted what any average man wanted: a wife with whom he could spend ample time after work, perhaps on a front-porch swing while watching the sun go down every day. I did the best I could in this way. I made sure that we had coffee together most every morning; I was openly affectionate with him in private and in public; we spent time going out to eat together; and we enjoyed day trips together. I gave him the best that I had to give, but I never pretended, lied, or acted like I was not clear about my calling from God—a calling that kept at-risk animals and children a very high priority. The times when my calling created moments of adversity did not affect my disposition in our marriage. Yet for my husband, these things could ruffle his feathers a great deal. My attitude did not change during times of deficit or prosperity, because I knew my "source" was unlimited. My husband, on the other hand, could only believe as far as he could see. Also, it was challenging for him to remain unmoved by issues at Noah's Ark, because Noah's Ark was not his dream.

When my daddy was alive, he was successful at helping us to band-aid our woes by putting his arm around my husband to remind him to "help support Jama's dream" because I was only the messenger. He reminded my husband that the "dream" was for all of us, and the dream could stretch far and wide, as long as we all believed. Overall, my husband did believe, and did not resist, but when it came to those little details in life, we differed tremendously.

Years later, there were times when I wondered if maybe my husband (and myself, for that matter) could have realized that we were getting involved in a marriage with an end date, despite the fact that we both vowed to remain together until death do us part. By most accounts, we had become two people who were dying a little bit inside everyday as our third decade of husband and wife came to a close. Surely I recognized this, even if I refused to see subtleties in the beginning that my husband would eventually want the Noah's Ark life to wane. Because my calling from God took priority, I believed that my husband would learn to adapt in full because of his devotion to God, too. Yet, his devotion to God with regard to marriage never grew beyond the traditional scope of the union. Surely my husband knew from the day that he felt so upstaged by the two white dogs who walked along both sides of me during an early-marriage walk that he had to call my momma about it that I was by no accounts a traditional wife. Something in him must have thought that in time I would settle down and reward him for his years of devotion with the sort of wife he'd always wished for. My husband might not have been the most extroverted, but like me, his yearning for what he truly wished for out of life did not calm.

And so there we were, two people who had hoped in vain for nearly forty years.

My husband's current perspective created a tension between us so thick that neither of us could continue to ignore it. If he was unnerved by something that happened on the farm that was either salvageable, or not at all deserving of his constant comments, he was consistently in my ear about how we would not be able to sustain our growing lot. I was able to rise above it, and did my best to let his comments fall into a box I never intended to open. But before I could ever put a lid on a previous issue, there were five more waiting in line. It felt like it would never end. I had to do something about it.

In April of 2010, I asked my husband to attend counseling so that the both of us might gain new insights to help balance our relationship. I told him that if he did not do this, I wanted out of the marriage. He knew how much I honored my wedding vows, and that to prevent a break in our union, I would put him above all. And by most accounts, he was right. Despite the obvious, I still wanted us to work. I believed that if we took the time to share our individual needs separately, soon we would be able to come together and thoughtfully combine our perspectives and thrive in a renewed way.

He later agreed to counseling, but not in the individual way I wanted. He wanted us to sit down together with a counselor and air out our grievances. I knew immediately that that would not work, because in earlier talks with my daddy, my husband would suggest that I was controlling our mediation. Those moments were intense for me, and I did not want to repeat them. I knew that my husband needed to feel heard, just as I did, and until the both of us could sit in a room together as whole, secure people, coming to an agreement would be challenging. In my opinion, individual counseling would help strengthen us, and we could have a better shot together. I gave him as many real-life reasons why we should not begin with couples therapy, but that only uncovered more wounds. This drama began to seep into our life at the Ark, which brought on heightened drama.

By the end of April, I told my husband it was over.

He responded by retreating. He took a job driving a truck and left for nearly three months. During that time he'd call, thinking that I'd changed my mind, and all he'd hear from me was more pleas to get counseling, or it was over. In my mind, when I told him that it was over back in late April, I meant it. His swift retreat that blocked any immediate action from me worked, as the time apart continued to soften my heart. He returned in August, and yes, I was eager to see him with a hug and a smile. The heart is very, very strong.

But that last trickle of possibility left in me was dashed after perhaps the smallest "welcome home" confrontation. To avoid more drama surrounding our marriage, I had to make a final decision and stick to it.

I filed for divorce.

Ideally, when one files for divorce, they are doing so to remove themselves from a continuous downpour of negativity, confusion, and emotional turmoil. When the marriage is over, said person might breathe a sigh of relief, having been able to move forward.

For me, there was no such sigh of relief. Because we were an admired couple by anyone who knew anything about Noah's Ark, the hailstorm that followed from our community was tremendous. And again, because I was the most publicly vocal of the two of us, the entirety of our dysfunction and demise was considered by others 100 percent my fault. If asked, I would never allude to or say directly that my husband was at fault for the severing of our marriage. I knew that we both had parts in it, yet it was only me who was willing to call our relationship for what it was. I took a lot of flak for choosing to move on without him, but to this day I do not regret it. I believe that we both served important roles in each other's lives, and I wanted us to move on separately at a time when we could still be in each other's presence without frowning inside.

In their own ways, our children and my siblings took the news very hard. Our children were already older with budding families of their own, but when you have no other vision in your mind except that which includes your mother and father together, this is not something easy to shake off. Peaches was especially upset, because I talked to her all of the time but never let on that there was trouble between her father and me. She thought of me as a hypocrite, and this hurt me to my core, but I believe I did the best thing to not be dismissive of her father while at the same time trying to protect myself.

My siblings were equally as disapproving of my choice during that very serious and vulnerable time. They took my decision to divorce very personally. I felt even more distance from my sister and brothers, as they believed that I had broken up my "happy" home. Despite any differences, though, I love my siblings very much, and it took time to heal from that period in my life.

However, close friends and those who lived in our home knew what was really going on. My husband and I did our best to portray a united front, but Paula, the only other adult in the home, knew how to read between the lines. Our foster and adopted children might not have been able to articulate exactly what tension they were feeling beneath the surface, but I never underestimate the power and intuitiveness of children. Additionally, every single animal I came into contact with (and I interacted with them all during various times) could also feel what was brewing, because the slightest touch from me would communicate my deepest soft spots. Jama the human being wanted to keep on the mask to prevent the inevitable scrutiny from family and friends, but Jama the servant did not fear the criticism; rather, she felt stronger with each verbal blow to her character. I knew what I was sacrificing, and whom and what I was sacrificing for. Noah's Ark was a vision that came to me when I was only four years old. I told my momma that I was going to rescue all of the unwanted and abused animals and children in the world. That declaration I made to my momma with my hands on my hips was one that spoke of a lifelong journey. At the time of my divorce, I was not nearly done with that journey; I had only traveled another leg of it. There was still more of God's work to be done.

God knows how much I valued, honored, and respected my marriage. To this day, I hold a great sense of reverence and love in my heart for the sacrifices my now ex-husband made for this great, big vision. We both knew in our souls, though, that his contributions had been satisfied, and now was the time for him to find someone with whom he could settle on a porch every evening, as he envisioned his life to go over time. For me, it was my opportunity to regroup and spend more time on my knees in prayer, because I knew that after the storm would come prolific sunshine for which I had to be prepared.

IX

Haiti

Looking back on my life, I had to know that the transition from torrential rain to prolific sunshine would not happen so smoothly. I have been blessed with untold miraculous occurrences throughout my life, yet those miracle acts from God often follow long bouts of faith-testing and faith-building. My departure from my husband was actually only the beginning of another level of testing my faith.

Not long after the divorce, I received a call from a pair of aging roadside-zoo owners in Illinois who wanted to find a home for one tiger and three wolves. I asked around to everyone who I believed could accompany me, but no one had the time. I figured this was God's way of getting me on a trip alone to be at peace with my own thoughts. The drive would be a long one, but I did not worry at all. I set my sights on the open road.

When I arrived, I spent a bit of time with the owners to learn more about their animals and collect any paperwork I might need. I had driven a large van with four sizeable crates to house the animals, and so I had prepared for each animal to ride comfortably. As I left, I noticed a tired-looking tiger in a secluded area, and I asked what was wrong. I was told that that tiger had a sickness they, the owners, could not diagnose, and because the tiger was covered in lesion-like marks, they believed that it was only a matter of time before it would die. I walked up to the tiger, and aside from it looking tired and having lost hair in some areas, I saw no other signs of extreme health concerns. I also saw the lesions, but they did not frighten me. This tiger reminded me of the tiny, sickly cat with eyes filled with puss that I tried to rescue when I was a little girl. Back then we had no stable home, and no real means to take care of it, so I had to let it go. Today, I had Noah's Ark and lots of resources, and I could take that cat home with me. The couple had not taken the tiger to a specialist because they could not afford to, and I asked them if I could take the tiger with me to be seen by our vet. I was warned that since I only had only four crates, putting a fifth predator animal in the van, which did not have a metal-wire partition, could be very dangerous. I reached my hand down to the tiger, and it sniffed then licked me. This gentle display assured me that the ride would be okay.

"I'll take her," I affirmed.

I drove from Illinois back to Georgia with three crated wolves, one crated tiger, and one noncrated tiger who had God-knows-what-rash all over it. Despite this, I still rode with a clear mind, and the long drive was just what I needed.

A few days later in a board meeting, someone commented on my arms, which were now covered in welts and a fair share of the same lesion-like markings. I'd been so busy, I had not noticed. The next day I went to the doctor and was diagnosed with ringworms. Our trusted veterinarian,

Doc T., who had not seen this sort of thing on a tiger before, deduced that I contracted the rash from it. Both the tiger and me were given human and animal versions of antibiotics for the ringworms, and within a week's time, all was well. I am grateful to say that Zuri, the name given to the tiger, escaped being euthanized, and is a happy cat today.

℘

About a year later in 2011, Momma announced she wanted to visit Haiti one last time while she was still strong and able to minister. She also wanted to travel there as a salute to Daddy. She shared this with our family around Thanksgiving, and while I was always in the spirit of giving to anyone virtually anywhere, I became faced with a fear that I'd never experienced: I was terrified of traveling to Haiti. I had no real reason to feel this way, but over the years my otherwise sheltered self had become privy to how alive racism is, and how fear inspired blacks from many nations to have a visceral, aggressive response to white people. Haiti was one of those communities. My parents had traveled to Haiti dozens of times throughout my upbringing, and of course returned home alive and unharmed every time. In fact, both Momma and Daddy—especially Momma—loved Haiti. What I'd heard from others about Haiti must have had a lasting, penetrating effect on me, to the point that I vowed to never set foot on its soil. It took a lot to get me to reverse my perspective and agree to join Momma. After putting specific prayer energy on the subject for the first time, all of my fear did not dissipate, but I became open to the possibility.

The trip was not long, despite a nice, touristy layover in Miami. Ironically, the closer we came to landing in Haiti, the less rapid my heart beat, and a calm overcame me when the plane's wheels hit the ground. Upon the opening of the plane's door, the Haitian wind hit my face, and I could feel it. I must have felt what my Momma felt all of those years ago when she, too, first arrived there. I was feeling the same inclination that motivated her to declare many years later that she wanted to minister in Haiti as a last major wish while she still had the tenacity to do it. When my own feet touched the soil, there was a knowing that moved through me. Haiti, just like that, instantly felt like home.

Despite the things I was told about Haiti, starting from my initial experiences, it took only a short time for me to refute those claims and rumors, as I fell right in love with the country. I encountered person after person full of pride and love for their country, but who were sad about its conditions. I met people who wished for a better life for their children elsewhere, primarily the United States, but if they could have it their way, they would all remain home in Haiti. I witnessed untold levels of creativity and spirit, and a willingness to work even in horrible living conditions. I watched people love and care for their children in the most desperate of circumstances, and for each and every father and mother and child, my heart ached. Despite the negative things people say about the people of Haiti, I have my own perspective, one earned through a raw and unfiltered lens. I knew that I could not fix all that I saw, but I clearly understood why my parents were so drawn there. They truly believed that if they were steadfast on behalf of the people, a real difference could be made. Although Momma told me her request to take a final trip to Haiti was for herself and the spirit of Daddy, I also felt that she was destined to introduce me to Haiti, as well, to pass on the baton of strong stewardship. Inherently she knew what the outcome would be.

On this trip, our company was Momma, Elijah, Sarah, Charlie's son Hudson, and me. A preacher to whom I was introduced by mutual friends served as our guide. He owned several churches in Haiti and allowed my momma to preach despite their rules prohibiting women preachers. I sat in the pews and watched my momma preach in full glory. She beamed while sharing about Ruth and other favorite stories of the Bible. The people received Momma well, and I became more absorbed within the fabric of the community.

After our first week of visiting churches and various orphanages, we drove nearly half a dozen hours to a particular location that housed orphans and women with children. Upon arrival, several of the women begged me to take their babies to the United States. Some tried to drop their babies in my arms and run away. At each request, I wept inside for each mother willing to abandon their newborns just so they could have a better life. On a later trip when I brought my son Charlie, a woman literally tried to hand him her baby while begging him through tears to please take good care of him. This experience moved my son so much that he could no longer return to Haiti. It pained his heart too much.

What can I do for these people? I thought to myself, fighting back my own tears. Just as I was thinking this, a motorbike pulled up carrying more people than I could have ever guessed would fit. Of the amount of adults on the bike, there was an infant who they shielded in the center of their huddle. They explained that they'd found the infant in a toilet. I was devastated. The baby, who had about five inches of hair, was covered in tiny lacerations, but was otherwise physically unharmed to the naked eye. My son Elijah took one look at him, looked at me, then pleaded, "Momma, let's take him home."

This is the beginning of what I can do, I affirmed to myself. It was at that moment that I committed to the abandoned baby boy. I'd always believed that I would be a strong voice for adoption, and as I had grown to love Haiti as another home in that short time, I'd been yearning for ways to help. What better way to aid than to show those who have resources that they, too, can help the children have a better life through my own willingness to take part?

I offered to take the baby, and all of the adults were overjoyed. Understanding the rules of adoption—especially international adoption—I knew that the baby could not travel back home with us at the end of our visit. The preacher friend of mine offered to refer the baby to his pregnant sister, who could raise my baby alongside her other children until his adoption process was final. She agreed, but on one condition: I had to adopt her unborn child, as well. I did not spend a moment to consider. I told her I would.

I later learned that my new baby, whom I named Caleb, was not the five-day-old infant I was told he was. I realized this because he fully lifted his head while I fed him carrot syrup and water. My guess is that his age was assumed by the people because of his tiny, four-pound frame.

To think, someone left this beautiful boy in a toilet. The

idea of it nearly broke my heart. I searched for the mother and she was found, saying that she left him there so someone would find him and provide for him a better life. I don't understand the logic, but if that is what she prayed for, her prayers were answered.

After about a year of going back and forth to Haiti to see about Caleb and his well-being, and ensure that his adoption process, along with his new brother's (who I named Joshua), was running smoothly, I decided to take a surprise trip to Haiti on my own. I had had enough of only hearing "word-of-mouth" about my boys. Having been to Haiti more than a few times by then and believing that I knew the environment well enough, I chose not to have a companion, and that choice proved to be a bit controversial. I was referred to a woman who held a few orphanages there. When she realized that I had arrived alone, she immediately sent someone to retrieve me, and upon meeting her, she escorted me to find Caleb and Joshua. Along the way, she had me visit various orphanages. In no way did I think I would be inspired to take yet another child home with me. That is, until I met Mackenson.

I introduced myself to Mackenson after the woman who owned the orphanage noticed me staring at him and suggested that I say hello. From afar, the little boy looked to be about three years old, but as I approached and looked at his face, I knew he was much older. When he looked up at me, I realized that he could not stand up straight, for there was a large lump on his back. His jaundiced eyes offered hints that he was losing hope; his blank stare communicated that he felt beaten. I could not cry in front of him, even though I wanted to, because I needed him to preserve the bit of pride he had left. I bent down and asked him, "Do you want to come with me to America?"

The woman who owned the orphanage told me that she would provide an emergency medical visa if I took him on my own dime. Without hesitation, I said yes. I learned from a doctor there that Mackenson, who was actually nine years old, had Scoliosis and was very ill. Because of my chance encounter with Mackenson, my trip was cut short. Thankfully I had accomplished what I needed to for my Caleb and Joshua, and I set myself on yet another mission.

I arrived home to Elijah and Sarah, who were excited to hear the news about Caleb and Joshua. I assured them that all was well with them, and that while on the trip I happened upon a boy named Mackenson who really needed our help. Of course Sarah and Elijah were all in. I looked at my children, who were seven and ten years old, and beamed. My momma and daddy believed in Proverbs 22:6 for me, and I have instilled this belief in all of my children: *Train up a child in the way he should go.* To hear my children speak so eagerly to help someone else made my heart sing.

☙

It was already 2012, and the past two years without my ex-husband had so swiftly passed by I could hardly believe it. I was given no real time to ponder the void of the divorce, and with Joshua, Caleb, and Mackenson, God had filled my cup three times over since then. In addition to expanding my family, I was doing my best to create some financial stability for Noah's Ark, which had been spotty here and there with money issues. I was always made aware of what was going on, but I have never been a stickler for it, and I have never allowed limited financial resources to deter me from pressing on to do what I felt in my heart was right. I had thought bringing Mackenson and his extreme health concerns to our home on my own dime would cost a substantial amount of money, but I never worried about it. I was blessed with a team of people who did not take advantage of, nor take for granted, all of our combined blessings, and this is why the Noah's Ark wheel remained well-oiled enough to function. While I believed adopting children and caring for their health concerns were the faith-testing experiences that would lead to bliss after my divorce, God quickly let me know that the summit of this test had yet to be revealed.

My trusted longtime business manager walked into my office in such a way as if she were hesitant to tell me the news: we were broke. I have been considered broke before, but it never deterred me because I was raised to be a survivor. The heat could be moderated or turned off to save money; I knew to keep the horses on basic food rather than sweet feed; and where there was a dumpster, I knew how to dive. But now with many more children and animals, Eckerds and the local pet-supply stores did not have enough "throwaway food" to suffice. My divorce was the storm, and what we were set to encounter was equivalent to the tornado that can follow.

My business manager told me that we'd been broke for a while, but she did not want to bring the news to me because I had been so focused on the animals and securing our home for the boys. She told me that sheer donations were barely getting us by. We needed to do something.

This was the very first time I thought, *We need to DO something*. Usually in times of crisis, my heart compels me to pray first. That prayer leads to an inclination of furthered action on our part. This crisis brewing must have been so strong that God bypassed the prayer part and drew my consciousness to the inclination of *doing* right away. Though I immediately felt the need to take action beyond prayer, I still knew that I needed to be guided as to what that action would be. I could not get down on my knees fast enough, and it hit me.

I sat at my computer and began to type the most difficult letter I had ever written to date. The thought of writing it gave me pause, and though we were suffering badly, I could not finish the letter. I did not complete it for nearly one month. The letter was addressed to a woman who helped us in the past with our miracle zebra, Evidence, and had sent in donations a few times before that. All of her former donations had been given to us without a prompt. Noah's Ark had survived through donations from people who'd helped without feeling any sense of obligation. I had never been in a position of waiting for donation compliance as a result of me asking for one. To me, it just didn't seem right. But this moment, I realized, was to serve as a marker for my life and all things to come; it was time that I learned and became comfortable with directly leaning on someone else.

Still, my heart beat a little faster than normal after I hit send.

Within minutes, I received a phone call from someone

affiliated with the kind woman who helped with Evidence. The day was Tuesday, and I told the person, among other things, that we needed $63,000 by Thursday. The kind woman's team member responded swiftly and wired the money the very next day. We then discussed a monthly amount to cover the key basics at Noah's Ark so we would never have to suffer in this way again. I cannot explain the sense of calm and security I felt. To know that my children and animals will not go hungry is something that makes me feel wealthier than any royal person. People like me do not need jewels and other extravagant things in order to thrive. Food, clothing, and shelter alone can inspire our spirits to soar beyond.

☙

It seemed like the gift from the kind woman could not have come at a better time. Caleb's and Joshua's adoption processes were still ongoing, but there was a sense of urgency to bring Mackenson to America. His health was in steady decline, and I did not want time to run out on him. After about ten months, we finally secured his medical visa, and I brought him to his new home with a prepared process waiting. Handling all of this was a layered task, and I am grateful to my daughter Paula for serving as my go-to source of support through it all.

The first thing we did was grab a bite to eat at Burger King. Mackenson loved it, but his stomach was not accustomed to the rich food, and it did a little number on him. That was my cue to be more mindful of his food transition process. Most importantly, we needed his health to head in the right direction. A physician I knew suggested a doctor in Miami who would perhaps take on Mackenson's case pro-bono. We drove to the location, and the doctor informed us after seeing Mackenson that he'd be better seeing a pediatrician. He then recommended one in Atlanta who he believed would take Mackenson free of charge, as well. We drove back to Atlanta and awaited the doctor visit there. All of the back and forth would have done a number on any feeble child, but not Mackenson. It seemed like once he realized that there were people truly rooting for him, his spirit soared. He was no longer the slumped, nearly lifeless body I'd met the year before. He was brighter, and even the yellowing of his eyes began to whiten.

The visit to the pediatrician in Atlanta taught us so much. First, after a series of blood tests with a separate specialist, we learned that Mackenson had sickle cell anemia. Then, it was suggested that he have an MRI on the growing lump on his back. The results from that test showed that Mackenson had a drip in his spine that was causing the lump to grow. My word, what a process this had become, but God led me to Mackenson because his life was supposed to be spared. All of this time with the back and forth would have amounted to quite a sizeable medical bill, but every single doctor who had encountered Mackenson had fallen in love with him, and thus refused to charge us full price, if at all. Therein lay Mackenson's grace. These acts of kindness were greatly appreciated, as his medical journey was far from over.

On one hand, I was supporting Mackenson's health rejuvenation, and on the other I was observing someone who had nurtured me transition in a different direction. Hank

McCamish, a great benefactor to Noah's Ark and a solid, trusted mentor and friend to me, was diagnosed with Parkinson's disease. His dear wife, Margaret, knew that it was only a matter of time. She comforted him from the moment he was diagnosed, and stood vigil for him until the day he died. Hank was a quiet strength who had a heart of gold that was open beyond measure. It was his and Margaret's benevolence that secured Noah's Ark as we knew it more than two decades before, and they then went the extra mile and educated me about how to keep it functioning well. Both he and Margaret opened their family home to me when I needed a shoulder to lean on, and they welcomed my entire family as if they were their own. Words cannot express the level of gratitude I have for Hank and Margaret McCamish. When Hank died, for me, it was the end of an era and the beginning of another one—one that embraced the future possibilities for Noah's Ark. Between Hank and my daddy, our Ark stood on some very strong shoulders.

Throughout all of this change surrounding the Ark, I did my best to stand strongly on the shoulders of the once-living angels who had passed on. I held tight to the gratitude for all of the positive things that no doubt those angels had a hand in helping: our bills were being paid on time, Sarah and Elijah were thriving, Mackenson had arrived, and the boys were on the way. I let out a sigh of relief for these good fortunes, and waited for the sun to shine.

X

Noah's Ark on a Higher Radar

During the summer of 2013, a dear friend of Noah's Ark named Susan LeCraw referred a couple and their two young daughters to pay us a visit, and they were entirely moved by what I simply considered to be "everyday living." The wife, who was a longtime animal advocate, raved about what she was witnessing, often saying throughout the day, "More than us need to see this. This great secret cannot be kept local." On their visit, they spent a great deal of time observing the BLT (Baloo, Leo, and Shere Khan), and they were in disbelief watching me, barefoot and with no protection, feed all of them in their habitat. They watched me feed wild, enormous predators raw meat with my bare hands and were in awe. They did not understand that these so-called predators were part of the vast number of animals I considered to be my "children with four legs."

Her husband was a filmmaker with various clientele, and one such client was a network called OWN, the Oprah Winfrey Network. The wife was also affiliated, and suggested to her husband that he shoot a short narrative about Noah's Ark for the world-renowned program *Super Soul Sunday*.

He loved the idea. They returned about a month later full of energy and questions. The husband paid such attention to detail, and the wife asked all of the questions they thought everyone would want to know. While answering, I asked myself, *Why would people want to know about me?* I was humbly flattered, but I was really doing what I, Jama Connor Hedgecoth, thought I should be doing since the time I had a choice in the matter. I never thought this would lead to people wanting to write articles about me and Noah's Ark, and each time someone wrote about me in reference to Noah's Ark, I could never fully embrace the attention. Still, never in my wildest dreams did I think I'd be featured on a platform as big as Oprah's! My momma had always told me that one does not always know what is in store when doing God's work.

When the show aired, our story was featured after a piece about a champion long-distance swimmer who swam from Cuba to Florida without the aid of a shark cage. She swam *all* the way from Florida to Cuba … without a shark cage. *Extraordinary*, I thought. When Oprah's voiceover began our segment saying, "Meet the woman who is changing the world one animal at a time," it was an out-of-body experience. First I thought, *My, what a follow-up from the long-distance swimmer! Changing the* WORLD*!* And then I saw my own face on the screen.

When I was a little girl, like many children, I spoke in superlatives a lot, using words like "every," "all," "everything," and "everyone." As a child I didn't know how much work it would take to save *every* animal or *every* child. As I grew into adulthood, I realized that the "alls" and "everys" take time to get to, if ever. I told my momma when I was four with my hands on my hips, "I'm gonna rescue all of the abandoned animals in the world." I know now that that might be the goal, but it will take, as Oprah so eloquently put, "… one animal at a time." The same goes for the children in need. I suppose one animal and child at a time can have some sort of effect on the world, but as I told the interviewers, I am only doing what I was led to do. I was in awe of my own self by the story aired on OWN. In less than six minutes, the filmmaker had encapsulated the core mission of Noah's Ark for millions of people to see. On behalf of us at the Ark, I am eternally grateful.

This level of exposure put us on the radar of people who had never heard about us or what we do. The BLT brought international attention, and people have traveled far from places like Europe and Australia to visit them. Having an endorsement from someone like Oprah Winfrey was a blessing.

Around this same time, a young woman who I'd fostered nearly seventeen years prior contacted me. She was more than eager to talk to me, because she was approaching her third trimester with her fourth child and she did not know where to turn. When we met in person, she confided in me that her three older children had become wards of the state, and she did not think she could handle the care of this baby, either. With tears in her eyes, she asked me if I would raise her unborn child.

First I asked her why she wanted me, someone whom she had not seen in seventeen years, to adopt her baby, and she said because when she lived with me, she was treated like a princess, and she wanted her baby girl to have the same life. I took a moment to weigh her proposal, thinking that I already had two adopted boys on the way with no full consideration of where they would sleep. My nearly four decades of motherhood to hundreds of children allowed me to make one more sound decision of yes.

Throughout my years of adopting, I've literally acted upon a feeling and moved on it. Paula, Elijah, Sarah, Caleb, Joshua, and Mackenson have their own remarkable stories of how I came to serve as their momma. When making the decision to bring them home, I never thought that time would be the last time. My spirit was still open. Yet I now believed adopting this young woman's unborn baby girl would be my last adoption. I had raised my four birth children, and now I had six more beautiful children from America and abroad to raise to continue to do good things in the world. *Train up a child in the way he should go.* This I intended to do. I would continue to serve as an example of why and how adoption for kind and able folks is a very necessary, and sometimes vital, thing.

Because of the young woman's vulnerability to substances, I asked that she reside at my home where I could keep a close eye and help the young woman with any impulses. She agreed.

Along the journey of her third and final trimester, there were moments when the young woman wanted to give in, and Paula or I were on hand to help her through those tough times. We offered to help her earn her GED, and as much as I believed she might have deeply wanted to balance her life, she could not pull it together on the combined support of others alone. She needed to tap into something inwardly profound that could inspire her to push forward for the betterment of her life. I had to readjust my focus on our unborn baby girl to ensure that she made it to the world unharmed. I stood by the young woman's side every single day until she went into labor, and the power of prayer was my strongest asset. When her water broke, I knew the baby was going to be okay.

In December of 2013, a beautiful, bouncing baby girl named Rebecca Hedgecoth was born.

※

In addition to having our story shared on OWN, Noah's Ark found itself the interest of a famed photographer. He called a few times without any reply from me because, honestly, I had never heard of him, and I was unsure if what he was asking was a real thing. I called my new friend, the wife of the filmmaker, because I knew she lived "in the world" and would probably know who he was. Right away she assured me that he was the real deal. He told me that he was preparing a book filled with stories of people who had accomplished the seemingly impossible, all by having faith. The book, in fact, was titled *Leap of Faith*.

He could not have been more gracious. He flew us to his home in Palm Beach and to New York City to be photographed and interviewed. Again, the photographer's team was very much surprised at how we had survived all of these years. Noah's Ark is a living testament to belief and faith. Since I was a little girl, my daddy taught me Hebrews 11:1, which states, "Faith is the substance of things hoped for, the evidence of things not seen." That, in a nutshell, is what Noah's Ark is all about.

When the book went to print, and I saw my family's likeness amongst others who are consciously committed to making a positive difference all over America, I felt humbled and proud. It was an honor to have key moments of our story be included and so beautifully captured on film, and that this accomplished photographer considered what we do at Noah's Ark worthy enough to share with the world.

☙

After that whirlwind experience with the photographer's book, it was only months before Caleb and Joshua were set to come home. I could not believe that after two years, our time to be joined in America had finally come. Looking back, I find it unreal how Paula and I went through trial and error without the help of any outside source to secure those beautiful boys. There was so much red tape, and many, many rules and regulations that could have soured even the most stubborn to halt the process, but Paula served as my lone teammate, and her support is what helped me to press on. All of this favor I continue to attribute to God's grace. I will never forget the journey, and each time I look into the faces of Mackenson, Caleb, or Joshua, I am reminded about why we fought so hard.

We brought along a team to document our final journey to Haiti, led by the filmmaker who created the short film for OWN. He also filmed Rebecca's birth in December of the previous year. Now that I had a documentarian whom I could trust fully, I wanted to be able to have some sort of moving account of my children's transitions so they would later understand how purposeful their joining with us really was.

Every single child who has come into my life has touched me in ways that make it difficult for me to express sometimes. I have four birth children, six adopted children, and over four hundred foster children who have brought me indelible purpose and meaning. I could literally line each of them up and have something personal to share about how I have been inspired by them. People who consider adoption an act of charity have it wrong. People who rescue animals just to think of themselves as "good" do not fully understand the point. In a humbled truth, we extend our hands to others, knowing the reciprocity that will occur when we open our hearts. Sure, I might have helped a lost soul or two or two hundred; I may have helped spare the life of an animal in my day; helped to extend a life; but boy, what I receive in return for the simple acts my family and I do pale in comparison to the feeling instilled in us. Every single living being at Noah's Ark is a blessing, whether two- or four-legged. Each day that I wake up, I am lucky to encounter these blessings I get to call by name as often as I want.

I am blessed, from my firstborn Charlie, to my last adopted child Rebecca, and each child and animal in between.

XI

Evidence and a Killer Goat

People have often asked me how I have been able to live my life fully on faith alone. I declare that I am able to do this because having faith in God has been the most unfailing thing for me. I have witnessed how having a steadfast sense of faith helped my momma and daddy get through the seemingly worst of times, and I have grown up feeling and seeing the hand of God working on my behalf. When people have denied me, God has always shown His presence. When people did not believe how far Noah's Ark would grow, I listened to the quietude of my inner voice, which told me that God always dreams bigger than any human being can.

Sometimes people believe that when they do not receive what they think they want, this means that God is not with them. If I listened to people, I would have believed that because my family had to dive in dumpsters for food, God was not with us during those times, that God had abandoned us. Yet I was taught to believe the opposite. I believe that God is always, always present. There are times when we are put through adversity simply to see how strong our will and faith is. When we decide to hold on and cultivate patience, we understand Psalm 46:10: "Be still and know that I am God." I have always believed that I was supposed to do the best with what I was given, remain humble, and God would handle the rest. Doing this has consistently brought me my heart's desires, even when these desires had not fully reached my consciousness yet.

This formula has been applied time and time again, but two particular experiences remain remarkably extraordinary involving two animals, one common, one not: a goat and a zebra.

In 1990, not long after I'd signed my name on the dotted line to acquire ownership for the Noah's Ark on which we live today, we found ourselves way in over our heads financially. I knew that the meaning of the tests we were enduring was to "pray harder, keep doing." And so we did. We were so caught up in *doing* that when a goat named Snowball was introduced to us by way of us learning that he was set to be mercilessly euthanized, we did not know that rescuing him would bring forth a blessing so big that everyone in Locust Grove could testify to the miracle.

He was called "Snowball the Killer Goat" because he'd accidentally headbutted his owner so hard in his stomach one day that the man fell over his porch and died. The owner's wife became instantly dedicated to killing Snowball. Her pleas and the story itself brought so much local attention and public outcry that Snowball was offered to us to see if we could rehabilitate and calm his aggressive temperament. Those close to the family told us that Snowball did not have a mean bone in his body, and his owner, now deceased, used to beat him with a belt buckle for the first two years of

Snowball's life in an effort to make him aggressive to protect the man's property. The day of the fatal headbutt was likely the result of Snowball having had enough. Still, the owner's wife vowed to have the goat "killed and put in her freezer."

We accepted the abused goat and I brought it to my home. Our prized veterinarian whom I'd just recently met, Doc T., covered my kitchen table with tarp and neutered Snowball right there to further manage his levels of aggression. We housed him near my home and loved him up while he remained sequestered for a total of forty days and nights. All the while, donations from all over poured in. I am not exactly sure why people chose to send so much money in the name of a goat who did not need much to live well, but I think they were thanking us for being so good to Snowball. The donations helped Noah's Ark tremendously, and though Snowball might have caused a fatality, he pumped new life into our world and kept us afloat for a time. After being sequestered, Snowball emerged and thrived as a sweet-natured goat until he died in 2001. We will always be grateful for the gift of Snowball.

About a decade later, Noah's Ark had grown quite a bit, and with new growth came greater responsibilities. Many of those responsibilities were financial, and though we were not in debt, we were close to flatlining again. By then I'd learned plenty about the world of nonprofits, including the fickle movement of private donations and how new levels of fundraising need to be put in place as an establishment grows to keep everything balanced. I have never been a fundraiser; I raise animals and children. I would work until my fingers bled to support my family, but I had never personally asked anyone for anything to help keep our boat afloat. But we needed help, so I did one of the things I do best: pray.

A few days later, we received a call that a baby zebra had fallen off a truck on Interstate 75. I did not believe it at first, thinking it was a hoax call, but when my office manager confirmed the call was from the Department of Natural Resources, I answered the call and drove to retrieve the baby zebra with Charlie and a young volunteer named Allison. When we arrived, the baby zebra was being held by a police officer who said the transport was likely illegal, meaning that it was doubtful anyone would come to claim him. I chose to bring it home to stitch up the cuts and bruises it endured during its fall from a fast-moving vehicle. I was shocked that a baby zebra that small could survive such an ordeal. Anything could have happened to it during the fall, but it survived. Looking the miracle baby zebra in its eyes, I chose to call it Evidence. For me, the zebra signified evidence of God's love.

When we brought Evidence home, I called our veterinarian to help, and she came right away. After stitching up a cut on its side, Evidence began to go to the bathroom. I watched it urinate from its normal designated place, and then I watched urine trickle out of the side where it had just been stitched up. I motioned to our veterinarian, who then told me there was something greater going on. She told me that during the fall, Evidence might have severed his urethra.

I took Evidence to a specialist in Auburn, who assessed the situation and quoted me a price. We were already extremely low on funds, and handling this case would have surely put us in debt. I called the DNR and told them about Evidence's issue and suggested that they pay the bill. They refused. So, I gave them two choices: they pay the bill and the zebra becomes a ward of the state, or I pay the bill and Noah's Ark becomes its legal guardian. They agreed. When our team began to talk about Evidence on social media, the windfall of donations was vast. Evidence's story continued to flood the social-media airwaves before spreading to the newspapers. The story then landed on the radar of a kind woman who, years later, would be the recipient of my very first letter personally asking for help. This kind woman not only donated a generous amount in Evidence's name, she offered build a barn for him to live in comfortably.

Evidence suffered various health issues throughout his short two and a half years of life, including having to endure another emergency surgery. He remained as strong as he could along his brief life journey, and he served as a grand conduit for more love and support for Noah's Ark overall. Like with Snowball, the love of God flowed through Evidence in our times of need. During both instances, I was particularly conscious of strengthening my faith, and the result of that was the miraculous experiences with a goat and baby zebra.

When one asks me how is it that I move through the world with a belief that cannot be challenged by any man, all I have to do is share one or both of these stories and they, too, cultivate a heightened sense of belief just by listening.

When we least expected it, in came God. But the truth is, He was with us the whole time.

Right: Margaret McCamish and Elijah

Below: Jama, Elijah, and Sarah

Above: Jama's five eldest children: Paula, Nicholas, Steven, Peaches, and Charlie

Left: Jama and Mrs. Connor

Right: Jama and Peaches

Below: The Hedgecoth children

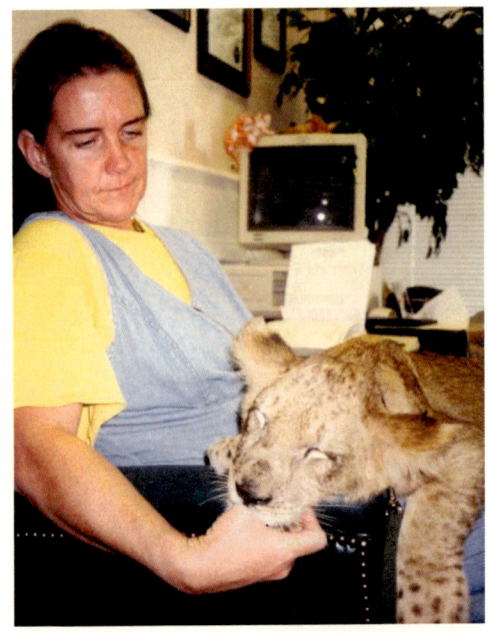

Left: Leopard cub sucking Jama's thumb

Below left: Susan LeCraw

Below right: Jama and Zuri

Above: Jama with a parrot

Right: Daddy (Reverend Connor) with a monkey

Top: Rev. and Mrs. Connor with adult Jama and siblings Art, Durinda, and James

Above left: (Rev. and Mrs. Connor) Momma and Daddy kissing

Above right: Jama and Daddy (Rev. Connor) at home

Above: The Connor/Hedgecoth legacy

Right: Jama's great-grandbaby Gia

Above, top: Momma (Mrs. Connor) in Haiti

Above, bottom: Jama with an ostrich

Facing page, top: Evidence

Facing page, bottom: Snowball, the killer goat

Jama and her children: Elijah, Paula, Sarah, Mackenson, Caleb, Joshua, and Rebecca in 2017

A Conclusion Worth Reading

Today, I am now in my sixtieth year of life, and though I have lived what some would consider an exhausting lifetime, I feel as vital as ever. My first set of children have all grown up and made their own ways in life, and I am grateful for that. All four of my birth children have moved away from home—one as far away as Hawaii! My firstborn son, Charlie, the one who gave me the most drama when he was born, has moved out of the house but only a stone's throw away from me. Charlie is my most trusted confidant and right arm. Who knows if all of this favor from him is simply payback for all of the stress I endured when being broken in as a new mother, but I'll take it! I am thankful that in choosing to serve on this road with me, God has blessed him with a wife and life partner, who happens to be Allison, the volunteer who helped us with Evidence. Allison, along with Charlie and my daughter Paula, has become a great asset to Noah's Ark. They care for these animals and children as much as I do, and with their support and unwavering stewardship of Noah's Ark, my heart is fully at ease with passing on this jewel of a place when the time comes.

The combined love of all of my adult children has always been a great source of inspiration for my sense of strength, and this helps with my younger children who, thank the Lord, are all growing so fast and well. Even with the daily 5:00 A.M. rise to get the day started with breakfast and school drop-offs, then tending to the animals, I remain young in spirit. I am proud to say that I am a mother ten times over, a grandmother thirteen times over, and I even have a beautiful great-grandbaby named Gia. Every day we bring home more animals in need, and with each one, I still feel like the five-year-old who smuggled a sickly cat into the back of my parents' old car as we traveled state-to-state saving souls for God.

Personally, I have lost my momma and daddy, the two most important people in my life who instilled in me to always do what was right and good and not worry about the rest. They were both laid to rest at Noah's Ark, on the very spot where I was first led to the land, and the same spot where I prayed a prayer that led me to a paramount relationship with our longest and greatest benefactors, the McCamish family. Hank McCamish, like my momma and daddy, has also passed on.

Noah's Ark has seen the passing on of a handful of other Noah's Ark supporters and family members, but in truth they are not gone. Their spirits linger amongst us, and sometimes their spirits can be felt. One such spirit, Leo, one third of our BLT, is the strongest. He presided over the Ark as our great king, and his brothers Shere Khan and Baloo have mourned him, yet carry on the torch of his presence within their habitat.

With modern technology, our process is evolving, like

our broadened reach through today's various modes of social media. However, our mission remains the same. At heart, Noah's Ark has always been a place where animals and children can go and be loved. We have since brought a close to the number of children we bring in, only because the maintenance costs were overwhelming. But where there is a will, there is a way. And my will has not weakened. I might not be able to house all of the children who need a loving home in the world, but I can serve as an example of how possible it can be for other loving, capable people to do the same.

As far as animals are concerned, the land on Noah's Ark is more than a small acreage, and as long as there is land, there will be a home here for them. I trust that God will cover the rest, as He has always done. We are tremendously grateful to the companies who have donated to Noah's Ark in kind, the individuals who make us part of their scheduled annual giving, and those who have given a few times. To those who are only thinking about giving, we appreciate the consideration.

I understand fully that Noah's Ark is able to exist because there are those out there who love children and animals. These people make it their business to support an organization that chooses to do what they cannot. These supporters get to live vicariously through we who work on the front lines for the animals and children, knowing that what they have given is spent wisely and honestly. We take nothing for granted, and know that miracles are what have kept us going for over four decades.

To continue on with our operations for more decades to come, Noah's Ark will always be in need of support in varying ways. In-kind donations are extremely valuable for those who reside here, and monetary donations are paramount to keep our team functioning. We will consistently pursue different angles to secure these needs, and will use mediums like social media to keep the public aware of what is happening at Noah's Ark. It is vital that support, be it monetary or otherwise, flows through. We are striving to build an endowment to prepare us for rainy days, and if one ever thinks that Noah's Ark does not need the support, my advice would be to think again. Animals don't cease eating, and they will always need health maintenance. So, as long as Noah's Ark has living, breathing animals, there will be a use for what someone is willing to donate.

When I lay my head on my pillow each night after I've said my prayers, what puts me to sleep are the recollections of the day and ideas for the new day to come. Some days are more challenging than others, but I can honestly say that for each life saved, each smile earned, what we do is worth it. I realize that I love animals and children so much that no matter what I did in life, I would incorporate them in it somehow. I'd find a way. It is more than a dream, more than an honor, to be able to say that loving animals and children is ALL that I get to do.

Afterword

by Chrishaunda Lee Perez

Animals, particularly dogs, have been a strong part of my upbringing, for I have an aunt who has always had a gang of them, and during holidays and summers I would relish in being surrounded by lots of paws. My family also had dogs as pets, starting when I was only a toddler. When I became a sophomore in college, I rescued a puppy and held onto her for sixteen and a half years. I have served as an advocate in various ways for as long as I have had a dog of my own. I have even cohosted a television show on PBS dedicated to strengthening relationships between people and their domestic pets. Every once in a while I'll surprise myself and do something extraordinary where animals are concerned, like the time I found an injured baby pigeon in a phone booth and I canceled a meeting to taxi it across town to the ASPCA. A reputation as a "lover of animals" quickly grew for me within the circle of people I knew. Yet, of all that I have seen and done in my own way, nothing could have prepared me for what I was to experience at the Noah's Ark Animal Sanctuary upon my first visit there in late 2012. And I have never met anyone who has served on behalf of animals the way Jama Connor Hedgecoth has. Jama is a woman I would not call a fellow animal advocate, but rather, an animal ANGEL.

That premiere visit there with my family hooked us all. I realized immediately that, even if one does not have an affinity for animals, what cannot be denied is the untold amounts of good that happen on the Noah's Ark Animal Sanctuary in Locust Grove, Georgia, and as a mere human being you want that sort of energy to prosper. There I spent time not only with dogs, but also with hundreds of animal species, domestic and not, and saw more than a thousand animals who all had an individual story for how they arrived there. It seemed like Jama had a connection to every single one of them.

Jama is completely unassuming. Her high-pitched Southern drawl, piercing, blue-green eyes, and signature smile welcomed us in before her arms made a physical connection. She comes across as a kind aunt you have not seen in a while who cannot wait to learn all that has happened in your life, never rushing to unload all that is on her plate. She does not talk a lot about herself unless specifically asked. You literally have to see her in action to gather all that she does on a daily basis. Watching her throughout an afternoon left me in awe.

During my very first visit to Noah's Ark, I watched Jama personally feed several of the animals, all of whom live on the grounds of the sanctuary (this included horses, cows, monkeys, and birds). I also witnessed her bottle-feed and give extra special attention to baby animals in her backyard, and walk barefoot into an enclosed habitat that housed an adult lion, tiger, and bear trio, holding a bucket of raw meat and a bucket of chopped fruit to feed them. She hand-fed each predator animal their desired meal until the buckets were empty. Then she sat on the ground with them and allowed the tiger to lick her hands. She even fed the bear a cookie from her mouth. After Baloo the bear gobbled up the cookie, Jama turned to me and said, "He'll do it with a grape, too." Having never seen anything like that before with my own eyes, I was rendered speechless for more than a minute. Even after I returned home and told several friends, I could not help but offer, "You really do have to see for yourself." I have since brought dozens of friends to Noah's Ark. They, like me, became instant supporters.

Before I visited Noah's Ark, I had not researched it or Jama at all. I actually took the advice of a friend of a mutual friend who'd heard that I was an animal advocate and suggested I visit Noah's Ark. It took a couple of months before I visited, and when I did, it was right on time.

Jama was kind enough to invite my family and me to the home she shares with her adopted children. The idea that she also provides the same level of tender loving care to children blew me away. I met Paula, Elijah, and Sarah, whose birthplaces ranged from here to China. Then I met a little boy she brought back from Haiti in hopes of making his stay in America permanent, as well. I became acquainted with two of her four birth children: her daughter Peaches and her eldest son, Charlie, who serves as her right hand. Taking in that Jama had fully raised birth children and was still raising this number of people did not overwhelm me; yet when she explained that the hundreds of children photographed and framed on her mural-sized wall were some of her over four-hundred foster children, I felt faint. Nearly TWO THOUSAND animals and over FOUR HUNDRED children? Again, for me, this was another speechless moment.

We conversed for about an hour at her cabin, and when my family parted ways with hers, I could not take her and Noah's Ark off of my mind and heart from that day on. Jama's family became extended family of ours right away, and all of our love grew stronger with each following visit.

I was so moved by the fact that she had found a way to provide viewing and quality-time access to so many beautiful animals to the public without a price tag attached to the visit. I learned that Jama, who grew up poor, did not want any child to feel deprived of spending time with animals as a result of not being able to afford it, as her family could not afford going to the zoo when she was growing up. Jama told me that she had living angels of her own who help her maintain her pledge's possibility, and that the well for feeding and caring for the health of any living creature is never ending; it needs constant attention and dedication. Jama does not say no to animals, and she does not say no to the honest benevolence of others who wish to support her God-given gift of keeping children and animals safe, healthy, and happy.

Thinking deeply about her legacy and the possibilities of what could happen if she truly chose to "share her dream" with those who had only known bits and pieces of the miracles that had led her and her family to the 250-acre farm in Locust Grove, she approached me to serve as her storyteller. This question was followed by a third speechless moment for me. I felt honored and humbled at the same time. It did not take me longer than a few moments to say yes.

During the two years that I researched and wrote this book, I have watched the tentacles of responsibility multiply out of Jama's head. I was around when she was compelled to make serious decisions that had to do with the organization and structure of Noah's Ark, and I witnessed the successful adoptions of three more children—two from Haiti, and the other from a former foster child. Two of the three children had to wait to be born before Jama could adopt them, and Jama personally nursed and coached that former foster child through an avoidance of drugs and alcohol to ensure a healthy delivery. When her daughter was born, she handed the baby to Jama, and Jama took it all on at that moment.

I have bared witness to the resilience of Jama Connor Hedgecoth, who, after nearly ten years since the "home going" of her father, had to also prepare a life-transition salute to her beloved mother. I saw the pain in her eyes for the sheer fact of having to let her mother go, yet, there was also a knowing that the spirit of her mother would always be there. Not long after, I watched Jama put down one of her four-legged children, Leo, of the BLT, the world-recognized lion, tiger, and bear trio. During Leo's demise Jama was at his side daily, encouraging Leo to walk when no one else could lead him to stand, hand-feeding him when no one else could entice him to eat. Jama then spent extra time with Baloo the bear and Shere Khan the tiger to help ease the sadness of losing their brother.

Jama handles both ends of the emotional spectrum simply as facts of life, and no matter what, no matter how dire a situation might seem, she always finds the good in it. This is perhaps the quality I admire the most about her.

Before Jama's mother passed on, she shared with me that Jama was a miracle baby, for Mrs. Connor was very ill when Jama was conceived. Seven months into Mrs. Connor's pregnancy, Jama's coming into the world was challenged again when Mrs. Connor was robbed at knifepoint. I took that as a sign that something did not want Jama to arrive in the world, knowing all of the love she would be capable of spreading when she did. Yet, God is a powerful entity, and stewards like Mrs. Connor, a petite powerhouse, were determined to bring her meaning-filled baby girl to the world safely, and she did. It seemed that as soon as she could speak, Jama began professing a life purpose that could only have come from a greater source. As Jama grew into adulthood, year by year, she fulfilled her end of that purpose, and the rest was met with miracles.

"Proud" is a word I would use to describe how I feel about having been Jama's storyteller. "Blessed" is the word I use when I describe our friendship.

My intention for helping Jama share her dream with the world is to inspire others to reach for their own dreams' possibilities, using Jama's testimony as an example of what can be done. Also, there are people around the world who, if they knew that Noah's Ark existed, and all that the Noah's Ark team accomplishes every day, would want to do what they could to help that goodness spread far and wide. Please welcome yourselves to the esteemed group of people who have helped to bring the Ark thus far.

I might have chosen to stop writing at a certain point of Jama's story, yet there are continued roads to walk, and hills to climb, and of course more stories to tell. In order for the wheel to keep turning, every little bit of support helps. Thank you.

For more information, please visit www.noahs-ark.org.

References

Bourn, Kathy. "Christmas Trees Get A Second Life At Local Animal Sanctuary." 11Alive.com. December 29, 2016. http://www.11alive.com/article/news/local/christmas-trees-get-second-life-at-local-animal-sanctuary/85-380208849.

Dilonardo, Mary Jo. "Leo, The Lion Of Noah's Ark, Says Goodbye." *Mother Nature Network*. August 12, 2016. https://www.mnn.com/earth-matters/animals/stories/leo-lion-noahs-ark-says-goodbye.

"Eagles Find New Home At Noah's Ark In Locust Grove." *Henry Herald*. April 17, 1991.

Emerson, Bo. "Noah's Ark: The Peaceable Kingdom In Locust Grove." *The Atlanta Journal-Constitution*. October 18, 2013. http://www.myajc.com/entertainment/noah-ark-the-peaceable-kingdom-locust-grove/AeW4NHFkhdtCnW6YKlNO7L/.

"Leo, Baloo, and Shere Khan." *People*. 2016. 72.

Middleton, Heather. "Animals Get A New Lease On Life At Noah's Ark in Locust Grove." *Rockdale Newton Citizen*. August 13, 2016. http://www.rockdalenewtoncitizen.com/features/animals-get-new-lease-on-life-at-noah-s-ark/article_bdaa0fb3-98d0-5257-9784-37084820dc54.html.

"Mrs. Hedgecoth's Ark." *Rockdale Citizen*. January 11, 1991. 18.

Osinski, Bill. "Bless The Beasts and The Children: Woman has a Double Mission." *Clayton New Daily*. April 23, 1997. 1B.

Perez, Jason. "Meet The Woman Who Is Changing the World One Animal At A Time." Oprah.com. 2013. http://www.oprah.com/own-super-soul-sunday/super-soul-short-noahs-ark-video.

Schmich, Mary T. "'Killer' Goat Wins A Reprieve After Ending Abuse His Way." *Chicago Tribune*. May 24, 1991. http://articles.chicagotribune.com/1991-05-24/news/9102160450_1_carl-hulsey-norman-sosebee-snowball.

Smith, Jason A. "Evidence The Zebra Debuts At Noah's Ark Saturday." *Henry Herald*. July 11, 2008. http://www.henryherald.com/news/evidence-the-zebra-debuts-at-noah-s-ark-saturday/article_c05b8261-c812-5338-b216-9bcc3b430080.html.

Smith, Jason A. "Evidence, Noah's Ark Zebra, Dies." *Henry Herald*. December 8, 2010. http://www.henryherald.com/news/evidence-noah-s-ark-zebra-dies/article_b9e88c4b-5776-5b16-9894-7d870eb50f20.html.

Smith, Jason A. "Noah's Ark welcomes wounded soldiers to Henry." *Henry Herald*. September 28, 2011. http://www.henryherald.com/news/noah-s-ark-welcomes-wounded-soldiers-to-henry/article_ddcc3154-2fe9-50a4-9c4a-17991d3d80b2.html.

"Snowball The Goat Put Out To Pasture." *Tulsa World*. July 8, 1991. http://www.tulsaworld.com/archives/snowball-the-goat-put-out-to-pasture/article_336f3fa0-73d1-5974-b3da-e29736a4ad2e.html.

Tagami, Ty. "Zebra Rescued Along I-75 Dies." *The Atlanta Journal-Constitution*. December 9, 2010. http://www.ajc.com/news/local/zebra-rescued-along-dies/eX80ysdS2CeAW7kiDu55QL/.

"'They teach you how to love': Meet The Lion, Tiger, And Bear Who Are Besties." Today.com. May 23, 2014. https://www.today.com/pets/they-teach-you-how-love-meet-lion-tiger-bear-who-2D79706596.

"'Zebra Dash' On Horizon At Noah's Ark." *Clayton News Daily*. March 24, 2011. http://www.news-daily.com/news/zebra-dash-on-horizon-at-noah-s-ark/article_2591dd5b-a99e-5434-a11e-2631662a0ace.html.

About the Authors

JAMA CONNOR HEDGECOTH is the founder and director of Noah's Ark Animal Sanctuary in Locust Grove, Georgia, where she lives with her six adopted children and over fifteen hundred animals. Jama has been an active animal-and-child advocate for over five decades, beginning when she was only a little girl.

CHRISHAUNDA LEE PEREZ is a writer, producer, and creator whose work ranges from film and television to print. Chrishaunda Lee is also a longtime animal advocate, and helping Jama "share her dream" has been a blessed and transformative experience.

For more information, please visit www.noahs-ark.org.